Dr. Michael Landsman

LORD,
INCREASE
OUR
FAITH!

BRIDGE PUBLISHING
South Plainfield, NJ

All Scripture references are taken from the King James Version of the Bible, except where otherwise noted.

LORD, INCREASE OUR FAITH!
by Dr. Michael Landsman
ISBN 0-88270-718-3
Library of Congress Catalog Card #94-070706
Copyright © 1994 by Michael Landsman

Published by:
Bridge Publishing Inc.
2500 Hamilton Blvd.
South Plainfield, NJ 07080

In society today, the forces of evil are arrayed against the nuclear family to cause division, strife, and ultimate destruction. In this setting, it is vital that we hold up Christian standards and contend for our families so that they can be all that the Word of God says they can be.

In this light, I dedicate this book to my beautiful wife of twenty-one years, Martha. Her love and dedication to the Lord and to me is a constant source of strength.

I also dedicate this work to the three greatest sources of joy in my life—my children, Michael, Linda, and Larry. They are truly a blessing from God and living proof that if you follow God's Word in raising a family, that family will stand strong for God.

Other Books by Dr. Michael Landsman:

Supportive Ministries
0-88270-702-7/Trade/ $2.45

The definitive text on the Ministry of Helps. Shows readers how to identify and fulfill the call of God on their lives. Excellent training tool and personal guide book.

Attitude of a Servant
0-88270-700-1/Pocket/ $3.50

A true servant is one who is determined to do the will of God from the heart. Through this teaching, readers can see themselves in light of the Word and develop the attitude of Jesus, the Servant.

Contents

Foreword

Michael Landsman has been a faithful servant to FFMWOC and to me personally for the past nine years. His life, in my own observation, has been a living epistle of a man of God not ashamed to serve other ministries and ministry gifts. He has travelled the world, imparting wisdom on many subjects, not the least of which is "the heart of a servant." He has loyally and faithfully left a good testimony of his own life as well as FFMWOC.

Oftentimes, people write books in an attempt to teach others what they themselves do not live. This is not true of Michael. His reputation and character are exemplary both at home and abroad.

His new book, *Lord, Increase Our Faith,* is yet another aspect of the "faith life" as opposed to the "faith movement." It will be both instructive and challenging to you. You will enjoy his scholarship as well as his practicality.

I heartily recommend this book to you for you to enjoy it, learn from it, and live it. This work is yet another step in fulfilling Michael's vision for the world:

For the earth shall be filled with the knowledge of the glory of the Lord; as the waters cover the sea (Hab. 2:14).

David T. Demola, Ph.D.

Faith Fellowship Ministries
  World Outreach Center
1994

Preface

The world is in a constant process of change. Momentous events are taking place around the world that are changing the face of the globe so quickly that many are left bewildered. Alternating feelings of joy and fear fill the human breast.

While we rejoice in the demise of communism, we simultaneously realize the tremendous price that it requires of us all. Is there any stability anywhere any more? Where can I anchor myself? How can I achieve peace and stability for myself and my family in the face of such cataclysmic changes?

We know our answer is in Christ, but too many in the Church today share many of the same uncertainties that beset those in the world. We know that our hope is in Christ, but we are like the father of the demon-possessed child in Mark 9. When questioned by Jesus about his faith, the father answered, "Lord, I believe; help thou mine unbelief" (Mark 9:24).

In Isaiah 33:6, we read that wisdom and knowledge is the stability of our times and the strength of our salvation. We also know that without faith it is impossible to please God, for he who comes to God must know that He is (Heb. 11:6).

Yet we are confronted with situations and circumstances daily that attempt to undermine our faith. We are like the early disciples who, when they were told that they were to operate in love and forgiveness, cried out, "Lord, increase our faith" (Luke 17:5).

This book is for the benefit of all those who are or have ever been in similar situations. "Lord, increase our faith in order to accomplish your plan and purpose in my life and in your Church."

Acknowledgments

In writing a book of this nature, there is the major source, which is the illumination of the Holy Spirit to allow the author to see the truth in a fashion that is uniquely his own. This illumination presupposes that there has been a constant inputting of knowledge to form the basis from which the Holy Spirit can bring it forth. For this reason, I wish to recognize those who have had tremendous input into my spiritual life.

The first and foremost is my pastor, David Demola, and his wife, Diane. Their example and care for my soul bring peace and tranquility. I would be remiss if I did not also mention Ray and Lyndie McCauley,

Rick Godwin, Malcolm Smith, Dick Mills, Joao Cardoso, Mark Hodgetts, Tom Deuschle, Gordon Calmyer, Joseph Prince, John Angelina, Leif Jacobsen, Richard Pennington, Richard and Joyce Tedesco, John Worley, and Andrew Sherman. Their love, support, correction, and direction have been a constant source of strength and inspiration in my spiritual life and ministry.

I also want to express special thanks to my publisher, Guy Morrell, and his great staff for their faith in this project, and for their constant nudging to get this book finished. Their persistence has finally paid off.

Introduction

Setting the Stage

I would be remiss in the treatment of this subject if I did not define from the outset the proper context in which we should desire that our faith be increased. The theme and inspiration for this book is Luke 17:5-10, with an emphasis on Luke 17:5: "Lord, increase our faith...."

In Bible school, my instructors taught us the following rule of thumb in interpreting Scripture: Any scripture taken out of context is a *pretext*. While this is a relatively small portion of Scripture that I am focusing on, I have been true to this little axiom in that the concepts presented herein are consistent throughout the whole of the Bible.

1

That said, let us discuss the context in which Luke 17:5-10 is found. It will help us to understand what prompted the apostles to make this request, and how it applies to the Church today.

FORGIVENESS IS THE KEY

> Then said he unto the disciples, It is impossible but that offences will come: but woe unto him, through whom they come!
> It were better for him that a millstone were hanged about his neck, and he cast into the sea, than that he should offend one of these little ones.
> Take heed to yourselves: If thy brother trespass against thee, rebuke him; and if he repent, forgive him.
> And if he trespass against thee seven times in a day, and seven times in a day turn again to thee, saying, I repent; thou shalt forgive him (Luke 17:1-4).

Luke 17 begins with Jesus teaching the disciples that it is impossible but that offenses will come. In John 16:33(b), Jesus stated, "In the world you will have tribulation: but be of good cheer; I have overcome the world." It is an established fact that we will face tribulations and offenses, but Jesus also warned; "...woe unto him, through whom they come!" It is better if we were drowned than to bring an offense. We must watch our own lives.

Jesus continued to instruct the disciples on how to deal with offenses. He stated that if a brother trespasses against us, we are to rebuke him.

If you're like most, you're thinking, "This is great! I can rebuke anyone who does me wrong! I going to give so-and-so a piece of my mind." That is not what the Scripture is saying. Notice the rest of the verse, which states that if he repents you are to forgive him. This tells me that the purpose of the rebuke is to bring a sinning brother to repentance, which is a change of mind that results in a change of behavior. It means to stop going in the same direction and turn 180 degrees.

When we think about a rebuke, normally the last thing that is on our minds is the reaction of the other person. To us, a rebuke is the opportunity to vent our anger and frustration at another person and to make them feel inferior or ashamed. Unfortunately, it takes the form of an attack upon him and his actions.

The scriptural concept of a rebuke is to present the truth in such a way that it causes the individual to see his error and to change his behavior. It is for his benefit, not my own gratification.

While Jesus hung on the cross, He said, "Father, forgive them; for they know not what they do" (Luke 23:34). That must be our attitude in dealing with the offenses that others bring against us. If they recognized what they were doing not only to us, but to themselves as well, they would not do it. (See 1 Corinthians 2:7).

In Mark 11:25 after Jesus has told the disciples that if they believed in their heart and spoke forth what they believed, they would have what they say, He said "And when you stand praying, *forgive....*" Forgiveness

4

is an act of your own will, not a feeling. You can operate in forgiveness even when your feelings are hurt and you are experiencing the results of offenses.

It is not enough that we are to forgive those who repent, but Jesus went on to say that even if the individual does the same thing to you seven times in a day and repents each time, you are to forgive him. Imagine that—he trespasses against you, he repents, you forgive him, the cycle recurs, and you must forgive each time. In fact, in Matt. 18:21-22, Jesus said to forgive seventy times seven times. *It is in this context* that the apostles, who had performed miracles to the extent of even raising the dead, said, "Lord, increase our faith."

1

Getting Re-Fired

In this day and hour, we, the believers, need to have an intimate understanding of faith.

I remember a chorus we used to sing:

We've come this far by faith,
leaning on the Lord,
trusting in His Holy Word.
He's never failed us yet.

What happens sometimes, however, is that we get weary, and we forget what brought us to where we are. God never wants you to retire, but to "re-*fire*." Sometimes we are more inspired by the Spirit of

God than we are at other times; when the inspiration is low, we need to re-inspire ourselves.

The Psalmist said that he made himself rejoice in the Lord—that there were times when he would actually *bring* himself to rejoice. When you have joy, you need to "rejoice," meaning that you need to draw on that reservoir of joy within yourself. Have you ever shaken a bottle of soda pop? The carbonation causes the soda to bubble up and overflow.

That analogy reveals exactly what we need to do sometimes. We need to rejoice and bring that joy within us to the point where it brims over, effervescent and overflowing so that there is no doubt about it. That is what we need to do with our faith as well.

The odds are that you are not reading something you don't already know. But we all need to be reminded and encouraged and re-inspired about these things time and time again. We need to be prodded into our proper posture every now and again. Our attitude must be one of positive assurance:

"In the name of Jesus, I will not back off, I will not give up, and I will not give in." We know that faith comes by hearing and hearing by the Word of God (See Rom. 10:17). *Faith comes by hearing and it stays by doing.* If we do not put into practice what we have heard, faith will leave.

The word "hear" carries three separate aspects:

1. to *repeat* what was said;
2. to *retain* what was said;
3. to *act upon* what was said.

Only when all three of these conditions are met has one truly *heard*.

I remember a time years ago when my wife and I were on the staff of a Full Gospel church. A very well-known preacher was scheduled to come to our area. We were all excited about going to his meetings. I remember asking one of the deacons, "Brother, are you going to the meetings?"

His answer surprised me, "Well, no, I've heard that message before." The well-known minister had been in our church about a year and a half before, and the deacon had heard him then. Because the deacon felt that the minister's message wasn't relevant to his particular circumstances, he didn't see the need for it, and so he dismissed it. The fact was, however, that he hadn't "heard" the message at all. He couldn't repeat what the man had said because he hadn't retained his message, and it certainly was not operating in his life.

Doing Your Faith

If you're not acting on what you've heard, you haven't heard. Many of us hear with our ears, but we don't hear with our spirits. We don't make it part of ourselves. Some of us think that if we hear enough tapes, or if we sit through enough sermons, we will increase our faith because faith comes by hearing, and hearing by the Word of God. I've heard it said that "faith" is a *noun* and "believe" is a *verb*. It's not enough to have faith; you must do something with it. If there is no action involved, you don't have faith—you really don't believe at all. If I have faith, then I will believe; and if I believe, I will do something. If I'm not doing anything about what I believe, I don't really believe.

For example, when I say that by Christ's stripes I am healed, even though my body feels contrary to that, I still have to make the attempt to get out of bed. I can't tell you the number of times my wife has said to me, "Healed men don't stay in bed." Our reasoning may go something like this: "Well, I'll catch my healing here at home." It doesn't work that way. Now, don't take this concept to masochistic extremes. If you can't possibly get up, you have no apologies to make. But there have been times when the flu would try to attack me, and my head would feel like it was swimming. It would take everything I could muster just to get up to go to the bathroom. But in spite of the symptoms, I'd steady myself, clean up, put my clothes on, and go to the office because according to God's Word, I was healed by His stripes.

I didn't feel healed. I sure didn't look healed. If you had asked anybody around me, they would have said that I was sick. But the Word of God said that I was healed. *The point is that I did all I could possibly do.* I put action behind my faith.

The devil once said to me, "How can you go into your office and counsel with people? You've got the flu and you'll give it to them."

I responded, "How can I give them something that I don't have?" You see, I *had* symptoms, but I didn't have the flu. It wasn't mine. I chose not to receive it. Make no mistake, however—I thank God that nobody came in for counseling, so they didn't have to stand with me! I remember those days well. Very frequently, my body would ache, my head would hurt, I would feel nauseated, and I would get into my office, close the door behind me, put on a tape, and just sit there and listen to the Word of God, following along in my Bible. I would just feed on the Word of God all day because the Word is medicine to my flesh. What I couldn't hear at the office, I would listen to at home.

SPEAK YOUR FAITH

We can see the importance of speech in Luke 17:5-6:

> And the apostles said unto the Lord, Increase our faith. And the Lord said, If ye had faith as a grain of mustard seed, ye might say unto this sycamine tree, Be thou plucked up by the root and be thou planted in the sea; and it should obey you.

In verse five, the disciples said to the Lord, "...Increase our faith."

Jesus responded, "If you had faith...." If you think about it in the light of whom Jesus was speaking to, this would strike you as a ridiculous response. After all, these were men who healed the sick, cleansed lepers, cast out devils and raised the dead. It looks as if Jesus is rebuking them, as if to say "Well, if you had any faith at all...." Some have actually taught that in this Scripture, Jesus was rebuking and testing the disciples to see if they *had* faith. This is erroneous.

Let's finish the verse: "...If ye had faith as a grain of mustard seed, ye might say unto this sycamine tree, Be thou plucked up by the root and be thou planted in the sea...." You would *say:* this is the point Jesus was making. Since you have faith, *speak what you believe.* "Speaking" is the proper action to correspond with your faith.

Jesus wasn't saying that if you want to clear your yard, begin to speak to the trees. Jesus is using a readily identifiable example, an illustration, to help drive home His point. What happens when you say that you're doing something? There is an action involved. If you had faith as a grain of mustard seed, you would *say.* What Jesus was conveying is that *the way to increase your faith is to use what you have.* In other words, if you want your faith to increase, use the faith you *have.*

ACTIVE LISTENING

The word "hearing" is an extremely interesting word. The word "hear" in the Greek means active listening. You see, if we

14

were to translate it correctly, it would read, "Faith cometh by listening," rather than by merely hearing. You can hear without necessarily listening.

The Greek word for "hear," precisely translated, means to be able to retain and repeat what was said, and to act on it. If I can't repeat it, I have not retained it. If I do not act on it, I have not really *heard* it.

DOERS OF THE WORD

Have you ever been to the place where you said, "I don't want to hear another message on faith. I've heard it all"? James 1:22 says, "But be ye doers of the Word and not hearers only, deceiving your own selves."

R. V. Transkar, in his *Tyndale Commentary on the Book of James* says that the word "hearers" implies that there were those who would constantly hear the teachings, but they never became true disciples. A disciple is someone who practices what he hears, someone who does what the Word says. But Transkar points out that James 1:22 spoke of those who thought that the hearing of the Word was an end in itself. In light of this understanding, it is clear that those who think that hearing is enough are deceiving themselves. Hearing alone is quite useless.

Some time ago, I preached at a church in Southern California. The pastor and his secretary picked me up at the airport, and I was very excited and hopeful about the upcoming meeting.

As we got into the car after loading my luggage, the pastor grabbed my hand. The secretary grabbed my other hand and they started to pray for God's protection from the airport to the hotel. Afterwards, we went to the hotel where I was to stay.

When we got to the hotel, I unloaded my luggage and checked into my room. The pastor asked, "Would you like to go for some lunch?"

I answered, "Great!"

In a few moments, we were back in the car. Once again, they each grabbed a hand and began to pray for protection again.

This went on over and over again during my three-day stay. They prayed for safety from the restaurant to the hotel, from the hotel to the meeting, from the meeting to the restaurant, and on and on. No matter where we went, anytime we got into the car, they prayed for our safety. By the time I left, I had become almost paranoid. I guess they'd never read that the angels of the Lord camp around those who fear Him, to deliver them, or that the angel of the Lord goes before us. They felt the need to constantly pray for protection.

Thank God, we don't have to quake in fear that way. My angels go before me. The angels of the Lord camp around me. Many are the afflictions of the righteous, but God delivers us out of them all. I have great and precious promises, and by these I become a partaker of the divine nature. My friends in California weren't praying in *faith*, they were praying in *fear*.

This pastor said to me, "Brother Mike, we just got these brand-new tape recorders that play at one-and-a-half times the normal speed."

"That's wonderful," I replied.

"Yes," he said, "I can listen to almost two

tapes in the time you normally listen to one. In this way, we're getting twice as much of the Word."

Then he said, "Not only that, but we found these new cassettes that are twelve-minute, continuous-play cassettes. They keep playing over and over and over again. We've put our favorite Scriptures on these tapes, and we play them all night long. We're getting the Word constantly, and our faith is growing."

I couldn't wait to go home. This was a genuine case of "weirdness" being misinterpreted as "faith." Never confuse faith with weirdness. Operating in faith doesn't mean behaving strangely; and faith does not come by hearing alone. There are many people in the Body of Christ who think that if they hear enough teaching, they'll have faith. This is self-deception.

Conversely, you have others who try to do things without hearing, and they fall flat on their faces as well. The result is Christians operating at both extremes and ending up with the conclusion that faith doesn't work.

Let me give you another illustration of

what I mean by this kind of hearing. My wife once asked me to go to the grocery store for her. "I want you to pick up this, this and this...." She rattled off a litany of things to pick up. My mind, though, was a million miles away, thinking about other things, but I was "hearing" her. When she finished, she said, "You didn't listen to anything I said!"

"Yes, I did. You want me to get...." Then I named everything she had listed. I got into my car, and drove down to the market that was just five minutes away. I walked into the store and got two items before I needed to go to the pay phone. "Now, dear, what was it that you wanted?"

"But I thought you listened?"

"No, I *heard*" I could repeat it then, but I did not retain it. Therefore, I could not act on it, and that is the true test of whether you have listened or merely heard.

Faith comes by *hearing* and it stays by *doing*. If you don't *do*, it won't *stay* You have to act upon what God says.

Some folks are self-deceived into thinking that they can just hear the Word, and the more they hear it, the more faith they will have. It is true that when you hear the Word, faith comes; but if you don't *do* it, out it goes. Sometimes I think that we ministers do a disservice to our congregations when we preach so much on so many different subjects. We never give the people the opportunity to do what they've heard. We have produced a generation that wants only to have its ears "tickled." They want to hear, but they never want to do. Perhaps we should start assigning homework!

Jesus went on in Luke 17:7:

> But which of you having a servant plowing or feeding cattle, will say unto him by and by, when he is come from the field, Go and sit down to meat? And will not rather say unto him, Make ready wherewith I may sup, and gird thyself, and serve me, till I have eaten and drunken; and afterward thou shalt eat and drink? Doth he thank that servant because he did the things that were commanded him? I trow

not. So likewise ye, when ye shall
have done all those things which are
commanded you, say, We are unprofitable servants: we have done
that which was our duty to do.
(Luke 17:7-10)

Now why in the world would He, in this
context, suddenly speak of having a servant
working for you? Jesus is still on the subject of faith when He begins in verse seven,
"But which of you having a servant...."
Now if the subject is faith, then the "servant" He is referring to is *faith*.

Jesus said, in essence, that if you had a
servant who had finished his appointed
tasks, that servant does not merit any
thanks because he had only done what was
required of him.

Early in our married life my wife and I
lived with a widow, and when we finally
got our own place, she decided to bless us.
She gave us a washer and a dryer, but the
dryer took three hours to dry a load of
clothes! The funny thing is that she never
understood why she always ended up with

poor-quality merchandise whenever she made any kind of significant purchase. It was because she gave only what had been leftover, poor-quality items that she received the same in return. This is a funny little anecdote, but it is a true story, and there are many people in the Church who live their lives in a similar way. We need to realize that when we need something, we should start giving it.

Years ago when I was leading a Monday night Bible study, my wife reached the point where she didn't want to attend any more. She said, "All you do is teach faith and healing, faith and healing, faith and healing." You see, that is what I taught because that was what I needed. I was sowing what I wanted to eventually reap. One fine day, I went to the Bible study sicker than I had ever been. I was burning up with a fever, and the devil said to me, "What are you going to do now?"

I answered, "Well, I wasn't going to, but I'm going to teach on healing tonight."

I'll never forget that evening. I taught on healing through a haze of discomfort. I laid hands on people, prayed for them, and God was healing. Left, right and center, people were having their healings instantly manifested. I, on the other hand, went home just as sick as I was when I arrived. I felt awful! My temperature had risen. As I laid on the bed, I remember the sinking feeling that hit me, and the little voices screaming in my ear, "Ahah, we got you now. We're going to take you down to the pit."

Instantly, seemingly from outside of me, I heard myself say, "He that descended also ascended on high and led captivity captive." It emanated from my spirit. The fever left me that instant! I reminded the devil that Jesus had already stripped him of everything he had. Jesus has set the captives free, and His power is still available to set captives free today. When you remind the devil of that, he doesn't like it.

FAITH IN ACTION

That is faith in action. I didn't call the Prayer Tower, and I didn't call the pastor. Faith is the servant of the believer. Faith is a tool placed in the heart of the believer at the time of the new birth for our use and benefit. God gave you the faith to get saved. You heard the Word of God, and faith came alive in your heart. You believed what God said, you acted upon it and you were born again.

Then God put in your heart the measure of faith. You can keep it at the same level or you can cause it to grow by hearing the Word and applying it. What I've seen happen is that some will attempt to operate above their level of faith. We try to operate above our existing measure.

People need to begin where they find themselves. I can remember a time when my wife and I literally had to believe for the money to buy socks. I can remember when I had to believe for a suit of clothes to wear. I was making $25.00 a week in 1972, in full-time ministry. The church's attitude was, "Lord, you keep them humble and we'll keep them poor." Several years later, when my salary had increased to $106.25, I "was called on the carpet" by the pastor. He demanded to know how I had

24

bought the car I had just purchased. "I know how much we're paying you," he squawked, "and I know what your payments must be."

Our payments were $135.00 a month, which at that time was a major investment for us. I explained, "I don't do it on what you pay me."

He said, "You must be telling the people in the church you have a need. I do not want you even hinting that you have a need."

I replied, "I haven't said anything to anybody in the church."

The pastor went on, "Well, then where are you getting the money from? The people in the church must be giving to you."

You see, the offerings in the church had gone down, and he was trying to figure out why. When I pulled into the church lot with my mint-condition used car his alarm went off. The truth was, however, that $135.00 a month was far more than we could spend. But what the pastor didn't know was that my dealer was a Christian, and he worked out the down payment and the financing for us. We never missed a payment, nor were we ever late. God gave me faith to believe for a car I couldn't otherwise have, and He made it all work.

God operates by faith. Romans 4:17 says: "...even God, who gives life to the dead and calls those things which do not exist as though they did" (NKJV). Why does He do that? Because there is enough power in God's words to make them become a reality, so where the Word of God says that by Jesus' stripes you were healed (I Pet. 2:24), then I can respond, "Yes, by Christ's stripes I was healed. I receive that as mine now, and I determine to act like it is so regardless of how I feel."

In fact, the best thing to do when you're sick is to pray for other people. Luke 6:38 says, "Give and it shall be given unto you...." If you need healing, give healing. A lot of us want to receive the fruits of faith without giving thought to sowing what we're believing for.

Faith is simply a tool for our use so that we can live victoriously every day we spend on planet earth. I don't know why people fight this truth so much. The naysayers call it "hyper-faith." Well, is it hyper-faith to want to live in the blessings of God, or to want to live in the prosperity that God says we can live in? Am I hyper-faith because I want to do what God's Word says, so that when adversity besets me I can win every time? If that's hyper-faith, I thank God I'm hyper-faith.

The origin, the starting point, for a true walk of faith lies in what we say. When you were born again, you did so by confessing that Jesus is Lord. Saying something, then, was how it all started for you, and your progress is entirely dependent upon how much of your vocabulary is substituted by God's words. When you were born again, you probably didn't look much different in the beginning. But you were, in fact, a brand-new creation. The old things had passed away and all things had become new.

The tangible differences, however, take longer to develop. It requires learning the Word of God and continuing in it. Most believers accept this without question. But when it comes to healing, finances and adverse circumstances, many Christians fail to apply this principle. Even when we don't "look saved," we can speak as a saved person and act as a saved person. Why, then, can we not apply this pattern to healing or prosperity? "If you had faith as a grain of mustard seed, you would *say*...." Speak your faith, the way you did when you got saved.

Please understand this about faith—it does not deny the obvious. Faith does not deny sickness when one is plainly sick. That is lying. Faith *responds*. "Jesus himself bore my sicknesses and carried my diseases, and by His stripes I was healed, and I choose to receive the healing power of God irrespective of what I see in my body, because His Word is true."

It all reverts back to the concept of changing our vocabulary. Don't lie. Don't deny that you're sick. Just say you're healed. Think about it—there's an important difference. Calling things that are not as though they were is a biblical practice. Once they "are," I don't need faith. If I've believed for

Getting Re-Fired

a new car, once someone hands me the pink slip and the keys, I can stop believing for it. It's sitting in my driveway. Can you see this distinction? Can you see where many of us have gotten into trouble and made fools of ourselves needlessly by misapplying the principles of faith? True faith recognizes obstacles and responds by stating, "But God...."

Romans, chapter four, says that Abraham, when he was over 100 years of age, considered not his own body nor the deadness of Sarah's womb. That does not mean that he didn't recognize it. It means that he didn't *consider* it. His wife was over ninety years old. They were obviously well past their child-bearing years. But Abraham pushed past the obvious, and he believed Him who had promised. God calls things that are not as though they were.

THE GOD-FACTOR

The angel of the Lord told Mary in Luke 1:31 that she would conceive a son, but she immediately regarded the circumstances:

"How shall this be, seeing I know not a man?"

God had plans. Our flesh causes us to impulsively overlook the God-factor. Instead of saying, "But the circumstances...," we need to say, "But God...."

I used to hear people say that they were operating in "blind faith." The problem with that is that faith is never blind. Faith sees clearly. Blindness is when all you see is what is around you. You are blind when all you can see are the circumstances. You see clearly when you are mindful of what God said.

We read in Mark 11, starting at verse 12, that Jesus was hungry. From afar, He saw a fig tree and proceeded towards it. When He got to it, He found that there was no fruit on it, and this prompted Him to say, "No man eat fruit of thee hereafter for ever" (Mark 11:14). The Bible says that the disciples heard His statement.

Now read what happened:

> And in the morning, as they passed
> by, they saw the fig tree dried up

from the roots. And Peter calling to remembrance saith unto him, Master, behold, the fig tree which thou cursedst is withered away. And Jesus answering saith unto them, Have faith in God. For verily I say unto you, That whosoever shall *say* unto this mountain, Be thou removed, and be thou cast into the sea; and shall not doubt in his heart, but shall believe that those things which he saith shall come to pass; he shall have whatsoever he saith (Mark 11:20-23, emphasis added).

Remember what we read in Luke 17? The disciples said to the Lord, "Increase our faith." And Jesus responded, "If ye had faith as a grain of mustard seed, ye might *say* unto this sycamine tree, Be thou plucked up...." Now in Mark 11, Jesus says, "...whosoever shall *say* unto this mountain, Be thou removed...." And then, "...but shall believe that those things he *saith* shall come to pass; he shall have whatsoever he *saith*."

Whether you realize it or not, you are

experiencing the fruit of what you *say*. Matthew 12:34 says, "...for out of the abundance of the heart the mouth speaketh." You are eating the fruit of your words, which are, in effect, the manifestation of the condition of your heart.

I know people who insist that every time they go on vacation, one of their children gets sick. Invariably it happens, and they think that they have successfully prophesied. The truth, however, is that they simply speak what they believe and then reap what they sow. It is similar to believing, for instance, that you won't have enough money for Christmas. You may go into the holiday season believing that you won't have enough money, and when that belief turns out to be true, you may think to yourself, "I knew this would happen." What really happened, in all likelihood, was that your unbelief and your confession sabotaged any possibility that your finances would end up any other way.

My family and I have been in such a position. But then we changed our vocabularies. We changed the sentences we said to ourselves. We said, "We have enough to buy all our Christmas gifts, and we will not have to do without anything we need." This affirmation replaced our earlier confession, "We don't have enough."

Once, I caught myself telling my wife, "Well, now that we have moved into this new house and have started making monthly mortgage payments, we can't go out to eat as much as we used to, and we can't do this, and we can't do that...." I had to catch myself, by realizing what I was doing, and this happened recently! I teach faith and I believe what I teach. But we all have to keep watch over our words and catch ourselves when we are opposing what the Word says. As it turned out, we were going out just as often as we used to, living the life style we like to live, and uptight though I was, I found that the money was there anyway.

Just as it is with anything in life, you have to start at the place where you are. You must learn, and build, and reinforce your faith to the point where you routinely see what you're believing for come to pass.

THE CONFESSION OF FAITH

Confession is not for God's benefit. Proper confession keeps your mind quiet while God is working. I heard it put this way one time: From the time that I believe that I receive until the time that I receive it, it is God's working time, the devil's fighting time and my holding time. You see, as soon as I speak my faith, and it is in conformity with God's Word, the angels of God mobilize. My confession becomes, in effect, their command. God goes to work, and consequently, so does the devil in his effort to get in the way. The factor that determines whether I receive it or not is ME. The lag between my confession and its manifestation is the crucible in which faith and patience are formed. We need to say what God says. We need to speak God's Word. This process develops the proper image on the inside of us.

If we are to operate in faith, our vocabulary has to change. We do not need to go to extremes, and fear for every little word we say, but we do need radical changes in our vocabularies.

Have you ever faced an offering where all you had was one penny and you didn't give it? Guess what—you sided with the devil. "But, Brother Mike, my penny wouldn't do anything for the offering."

You're right. It wouldn't affect the offering at all. But it does affect the image of God in you, because Second Corinthians 9:8 says, "And God is able to make all grace [every favor and earthly blessing] come to you in abundance, so that you may always and under all circumstances and whatever the need, be self-sufficient- —possessing enough to require no aid or support and furnished in abundance for every good work and charitable donation" (TAB).

If I have a penny, I have enough. When the offering comes by, give a penny if all you have is a penny, because God said that I have enough for every good work and charitable donation. And when I put that penny in, I say, "Devil, the Word of God says that I always have enough for every good work and charitable donation, and in the name of Jesus, there it is. You can't stop me because God says it."

That is the image of God in me. I always have enough. Does that penny affect the offering? No. Does it affect you? Tremendously, because you have now operated in line with the Word of God and you say with your mouth that which you believe in your heart. Even if it is only a penny, the Word says it is enough.

2

Issuing Commands
by Faith

There is another perspective from which we can view our incredibly rich foundational text (Luke 17). It involves the people who were asking Jesus to increase their faith.

> Then he called his twelve disciples together, and gave them power and authority over all devils, and to cure diseases. And he sent them to preach the kingdom of God, and to heal the sick....And they departed, and went through the towns, preaching the gospel, and healing every where (Luke 9:1-2,6).

> And when he had called unto him
> his twelve disciples, he gave them
> power against unclean spirits, to cast
> them out, and to heal all manner of
> sickness and all manner of disease
> (Matt. 10:1).
>
> After these things the Lord appoint-
> ed other seventy also, and sent them
> two and two before his face into ev-
> ery city and place, whither he him-
> self would come.... And the seventy
> returned again with joy, saying,
> Lord, even the devils are subject
> unto us through thy name (Luke
> 10:1,17).

Now here are individuals who have gone
out and healed the sick, cleansed lepers,
raised the dead and cast out devils. Talk
about an exciting time! These men returned
from doing all these miraculous exploits,
and they asked, "Lord, increase our faith."
Imagine that.

Notice that Jesus, when He sent the disciples forth did not say, "Pray and ask God
to heal them."

Rather, Luke 9:1 says that He gave *them* power and authority over all devils and to cure diseases; and He sent them to preach the gospel.

What did He send them to do? To preach and to heal. He gave the disciples, individually and personally, the power to cure diseases, cast out devils and all the rest. That same command issues down to us today.

So often we ask God to do what He has already commanded us to do for ourselves. Have you ever tried to get someone else to do your work for you? My son likes to do that. I'll give him something to do, then he'll come back a few minutes later pleading ignorance in an effort to ultimately get me to do what I've asked of him under the guise of "showing him how."

THE BLESSING WILL OVERTAKE YOU

As Christians, we sometimes do the same sort of thing. We do not usually do so out of duplicity or malice, but only out of a lack of understanding of the commission of Jesus and of the principles of faith. Too many of us have the false idea that God wants us to build this tremendous faith in us so that He can bless us. Consequently, all of our aspirations in exercising our faith are misdirected and are for the purpose of obtaining things for us, rather than to meet the needs of others. Consider this oft-quoted Scripture:

> And it shall come to pass, if thou shalt harken diligently unto the voice of the Lord thy God, to observe and to do all his commandments which I command thee this day, that the Lord thy God will set thee on high above all nations of the earth: And all these blessings shall come on thee, and overtake thee, if thou shalt hearken unto the voice of the Lord thy God (Deut. 28:1-2).

You cannot be overtaken by something you are pursuing for yourself. Matthew 6:33 says, "But seek ye first the kingdom of God, and his righteousness; and all these things shall be added unto you." We spend great amounts of time doing what we think is seeking the kingdom of God, and nothing ever seems to be added to us. Have you noticed that?

Have you ever found yourself doing what you thought was seeking the kingdom of God and nothing was added unto you? What we used to think "seeking the Kingdom of God" meant was prayer and study of the Word. In actual fact, the word "kingdom," in the original language, means the activity of reigning. For the believer, the activity of reigning is broken down into three aspects: bringing deliverance to the captives; exerting authority over the enemy; and conferring blessings upon God's people. So if I am truly seeking first the Kingdom of God, what I am doing is bringing deliverance, exercising my authority over the enemy, and blessing God's people. Only then am I seeking first the kingdom of God.

Yes, study and prayer are essential because I must have something to give those to whom I minister, but seeking first the kingdom means to be actively reigning with authority over what God has given to me.

Another Scripture many people love is 2 Timothy 2:15, "Study to shew thyself approved unto God, a workman that needeth not to be ashamed, rightly dividing the word of truth." That's a wonderful Scripture, and we understand the word "study" to mean surrounding ourselves with our lexicons and concordances, and to run references, and to find out the Greek meaning of this and the Hebrew meaning of that, all in an effort to show ourselves approved. Then we can stand assured that we can quote chapter and verse with the best of them.

My brother and sister, I don't want just to know chapter and verse—I want it working in my life. It's great to know chapter and verse, but if what you're studying is not operating and evident in your life, you're wasting your time.

The word "study" comes from a Middle English word, and it does not refer to "studying" as we know it. It means to be actively involved in doing what you know is right. The New King James Version gives us a clearer understanding of the meaning when it says, "Be *diligent* to show yourself approved."

FAITH STAYS BY DOING

Therefore, "seeking first the kingdom of God" and "studying" involve, by and large, the same concept—to be actively involved in doing what you know is right: bringing deliverance, exercising authority and conferring blessing. *As you involve yourself with these pursuits, you are rightly dividing the Word of truth.* This does not mean only that you are to rightly divide the Word to know right from wrong. God wants you to rightly divide the Word so you can *do* it. We have erroneously centered all of our attention on knowing the difference between right and wrong and we've stopped there. We love to camp around Romans 10:17, "So then faith cometh by hearing, and hearing by the Word of God," and we tell ourselves, "Faith comes by hearing, and hearing, and hearing...." We get so excited about hearing the Word of God, buying tapes, running to hear this preacher and that one. But in the pursuit of hearing, too many of us have forgotten the *doing*. We think that the hearing is an end in itself. It is more accurate to state, *faith comes by hearing and it stays by doing.*

I have no problem believing that faith comes by hearing. Every time the Word of God is preached, faith comes. But it is not enough for faith simply to come. I don't want it to come and go. We've majored so much on hearing that we've become spiritually obese and atrophied due to much consumption and no activity. When you know to do the Word as you seek first the kingdom, and you've done all you know to do, exercised all the faith you can muster, and you are operating at or near capacity in your Christian service, what do you do next?

This question takes us back to our text in Luke 17, because the apostles had similar questions. They asked of Jesus, "Lord, increase our faith, increase our capacity; we want to be able to do more." Recall that the Lord responded, "If you had faith...." *No one would ask you to increase something you didn't already have.* If they didn't have faith, why would they have asked Jesus to increase it? The point is that the apostles already had what they were asking for. That is why Jesus said to use what you have—because what you have is sufficient for the task at hand.

The apostles implored, "Lord, increase our faith," and He responded, "If you had faith as a grain of mustard seed." They had faith. All they asked for was that it be increased. The incredible exploits that they had accomplished proved them to be men of faith. So when Jesus said, "*If* you had faith as a grain of mustard seed...," He was not rebuking them, but rather showing them how to go about increasing their faith. "Say unto the sycamine tree, Be thou plucked up by the root, and be thou planted in the sea; and it should obey you." Jesus was saying that the way to go about increasing your faith is first by doing something with the faith you have. If you had faith, you would *say*—you would do something with it.

Secondly, in order for our faith to grow, we must know *what* to say—we must change our vocabulary. Jesus was not giving a discourse on how to talk to trees. His intention was not for you and I to go around talking to vegetation. Our vocabularies must change. Why? Because what we say must conform with what God has said. It's not about speaking your mind. If you want results, you'll speak God's mind, which is His Word.

Romans 3:4 says,

> ...let God be true, but every man a
> liar,...That thou mightest be justified
> in thy sayings, and mightest over-
> come when thou art judged.

Anyone who speaks contrary to what God said is lying. And how is one justified in his sayings? By saying what God says. If I say what God says, then I am justified in what I say and then I will overcome when I am condemned (judged), and you WILL be condemned (judged). When you start speaking what God says, you can expect to be ridiculed. But the people that condemn and ridicule you simply don't understand. They probably don't do it maliciously, and we need to avoid responding maliciously. Such responses are unprofitable and immature. What the naysayers proclaim shouldn't affect what you believe. If people want to think I'm a nut, let them. I'm still going to love them, and pray for them, and minister to them. I refuse to be moved.

I worked with the Los Angeles Police Department for five and a half years as a chaplain, and if you think I don't know about being the brunt of jokes, please think again. I remember the first time I had to talk a jumper off a bridge. All I did was preach the Word to him, and all he said was, "I'm going to jump."

I said, "No, you're going to come down here and I'm going to tell you about Jesus."

And he said, "No."

They were using bullhorns in their efforts to get through to this fellow, but they got nowhere. I put the bullhorn aside and just started preaching to him. He came down from his perch, walked off the bridge, and I walked with him a half mile, telling him about Jesus all the way. You talk about a laughing stock; the guys on the department couldn't seem to talk about anything else. "If I'd been him, I would have jumped" was the type of abuse I was subjected to. But you see, I knew then that it was the best thing that could have happened, because in their world, making jokes about someone was their way of communicating acceptance. They accepted me. They were happy that they didn't have to climb up there to try to get him. If I hadn't talked him down, that would have been the next step. Every time there was a similar incident after that, they'd call me. We had three chaplains in our division, but they called me because things seemed to happen when I showed up. My prayers seemed to work.

Things would quiet down when I came on the scene, and I acquired a reputation. They thought I was nuts, but they knew that *somehow* what I believed, taught and lived actually worked. I was invited to all the parties, picnics and functions that other cops were invited to.

48

It's so important for us to change what we normally say when sickness and disease attach themselves to our bodies. Do we deny that we are sick? No, because that is lying. Faith does not lie. Well then, what do you say? Try this: "Jesus himself bore my sicknesses and carried my diseases, and by His stripes I am healed; I choose to line up with what God says."

We need to determine where we are in our faith, operate within that level, and grow from there. *Too frequently, people fail to honestly assess themselves, and so they try to operate on a level above their actual faith level and consequently they embarrass themselves because they step out in presumption, not faith.* They operate on someone else's experience, and it does not work for them.

Once, when I broke my ankle, my faith was at the point of knowing the doctor would do an excellent job of setting the bone, but I had faith for little more. I was not at the place where I could just get up and walk. "Well, Brother Mike, is that operating in faith?" someone may ask.

Absolutely. You'd better believe I operated in faith in that situation. I honestly assessed where I was, and I exercised the faith I had.

I have grown in my faith since then. At that time, I didn't have what I have now. But I used what I had.

When we first moved to New Jersey, we needed to buy a new car. I was presented with the opportunity to buy a luxury car. I certainly could have afforded it. I looked at the price of the car and the amount of the payments. I then looked at an Oldsmobile, the cost, the payments, and all the rest, and I opted for the Oldsmobile. I could have bought the luxury car without any problem, but I chose instead to save the extra money to put towards other things.

I stepped out in what I believed was God, and as a result of that decision, tremendous things happened for my family and me within the next eighteen months.

FAITH, NOT ACCEPTANCE

For example, we were able to purchase a beautiful home. While some may criticize and say that I displayed a lack of faith in not opting for the car I desired, the bottom line is that I operated within my own level of faith, and God honored it.

Do not confuse recognition of where you are in your faith with *acceptance*. We should never be content with where we are. We must follow the apostles' example: "Lord, increase our faith."

Once you've established your faith level, you need to remember to save yourself some time and hassle by realizing that when you begin to change the way you talk, you open yourself up for ridicule and persecution from your friends. It will not come from your enemies. Real persecution very seldom comes from your enemies. It comes from Christian brothers and sisters who don't understand. We, however, sometimes make absurd statements that expose us to ridicule, and rightly so.

Some years ago, I went to an exclusive department store with a minister friend of mine in Southern California to look at suits. Neither of us saw anything we particularly cared for, and as we were making our way out of the shop, the salesman, who had been very helpful, said, "Take care" in a very friendly manner. My friend turned around and, at the top of his lungs in the middle of

51

this very elegant store, shouted, "No, thank you. I don't have a care. I refuse to take a care. I cast all my cares upon the Lord because He careth for me." I cringed inside and I wanted to hide. My friend's exclamation called attention not to the gospel, but to himself. Shoppers all around gawked at us in bewilderment, and I'm sure they questioned my companion's sanity.

People often try to corner me into "being real." Their assumption is that my faith-walk is phony. In the dead of winter, they'll ask me, "Aren't you afraid you're going to catch something?"

My response is always the same: "No." If they press me further, they might challenge, "How can you be so sure you're not going to catch the flu?"

Think about this mentality for a moment. In order for me to catch a football, I must get my hands in a position to catch it. To catch a baseball, I've got to stick the mitt up to catch it. *I refuse to actively pursue what the devil has for me.* I'm not going to catch it. It doesn't mean it won't try to come on me, but I'm not going to stick my mitt up for it.

If symptoms come, I'm going to stand against them with the Word of God. In verse 7 we read about the servant. Remember that the context in which we read this parable involves increasing faith. Jesus said,

> But which of you, having a servant plowing or feeding cattle, will say unto him by and by, when he is come from the field, Go and sit down to meat.

In other words, after the servant has done all of his work in the field and comes in, do you tell the servant to sit down and proceed to wait on him? No. Jesus said,

> And will not rather say unto him, Make ready wherewith I may sup, and gird thyself and serve me, till I have eaten and drunken; and afterward thou shalt eat and drink? Doth he thank that servant because he did the things that were commanded him? I trow not. So likewise ye, when ye

53

shall have done all those things which are commanded you, say, We are unprofitable servants: we have done that which was our duty to do (Luke 17:8-10).

Faith is a servant to the believer. Let me put it in terms that you may find more palatable than "servant." Faith is a tool. You don't honor tools—you use them. I don't take my power drill and say, "Behold this wonder. It can screw screws into a wall, and it can reverse and take the screws out. It can drill holes in metal. Let us build a memorial." You use a drill for the task at hand, and you expect it to work. Otherwise, you'll take it back to the store and get one that does work.

But, what do we do with faith? "Look what I got by my faith. I got a new car with my faith, a new house, new clothes. See what my faith has done?" For too many of us, faith, which has been given to us as a tool for service, has become an idol—an end in itself. Faith is not to be worshiped. We are to worship the Father, the Son and the

Holy Spirit, and God has given us faith so that we can live victoriously in this life. This is what Jesus is teaching in verse 7. Faith has been given to us to use, not to run after.

The parable of the servant in Luke 11 yields another lesson. What compels a servant to follow orders? *A servant responds not to words or commands themselves, but to the authority behind them.* The servant's orders came from one higher in authority than he. The same words spoken by someone with no authority would bring about a much different response. But the servant's master issued words, which were a command, and they were obeyed. Isaiah 55:11 says,

> So shall my word be that goeth forth out of my mouth: it shall not return unto me void, but it shall accomplish that which I please, and it shall prosper in the thing whereto I sent it.

Why? Because God's Word is alive, active, and full of power—as it says in Hebrews 4:12. Residing within the Word of

God is all the power necessary to bring it to pass; but it takes an obedient servant to obey the command.

One such command is found in Mark 16:18: "...lay hands on the sick, and they shall recover." The power to bring healing and recovery is inherent in the command. And when we execute the command, it works. We can stare at the command, debate it, and look up the meaning of each of the words and study them, but it will never happen in our lives until we obey the command. Jesus said that faith is like the servant who obeys the command. Give it the command and watch it work. *We* must issue the commands. God has left the controls in our hands.

> And I will give unto thee the keys of the kingdom of heaven: and whatsoever thou shalt bind on earth shall be bound in heaven: and whatsoever thou shalt loose on earth shall be loosed in heaven (Matt. 16:19).

"Where the word of a king is, there is

power: and who may say unto him, What doest thou?" (Eccles. 8:4).

AUTHORITY TO COMMAND

We must learn that we have the authority to issue commands. Psalm 103:20 says, "Bless the Lord, ye his angels, that excel in strength, that do his commandments, hearkening unto the voice of his word." Angels hearken unto the voice of the Word to do the commandments.

Who gives voice to those words or those commandments? You do. When you say, "Be healed," the angels hearken to the voice of the Word. All the power that is necessary to bring it to pass comes into play. What many fail to realize is that authority is never vested in an individual. *Rather, authority is vested in a position.* When an individual assumes a certain position, he then possesses the authority that position carries. Therefore, it is the responsibility of the individual to do what he must to assume the position necessary to wield the authority he seeks.

No one is born with the power to deploy the nation's military forces. You must first become the president, the commander-in-chief. Ask yourself, "Did you have power over the devil before you got saved?" The answer is clearly no. But that changed after you were saved. What happened? What made the difference? It was the authority; you changed positions. "Who hath delivered us from the power of darkness, and hath translated us into the Kingdom of his dear Son" (Col. 1:13). God took us out of the control and dominion of darkness; then He placed us in the kingdom of His dear Son.

When I was born again, I changed positions. Do I now have authority because of *me?* No! I have authority because of the position I am in. The authority is in my position in Christ; it's not in me. As long as I am in this position, I can exercise authority over the devil, over sickness, over poverty and over all things. Angels hearken unto the voice of the Word when I speak it. According to Hebrews 1:14, angels are ministering spirits sent forth to minister for them who are the heirs of salvation. You are not an heir until you get into the family. When you get a handle on what I'm trying to convey, you'll see that faith is not such a mystical concept, and you'll see it for what it really is—a response to the command of God. And then, because these commands are God's words, things happen. God's Word does not return unto Him void. Psalm 89:34 says, "My covenant will I not break, nor alter the thing that is gone out of my lips." Yet Christians spend a great deal of time attempting to explain why it will not work. If you want to get into an argument quickly, suggest to a believer that his faith needs to increase. It works every time. That is because this suggestion would imply that his unanswered prayer might have something to do with *Him*. It's like a person who overspends constantly until he is very deeply in debt, but he can't understand why because he only spends money on "bare necessities," i.e., eating out twice a week, a trip to the local department store every other week, etc. Surely, he couldn't be overspending! We have raised multiple generations of Christians to believe that whatever God wants to do is okay, and that we must "play the hand we're dealt," and move on. The trouble with that philosophy is that it has not occurred to enough Christians that the adversity they're facing often bears no resemblance to God's will for their lives. In Isaiah 45:11 God said, "...concerning the work of my hands command ye me." When you place a demand upon what God has said, you'll get results.

In the naysayers' favorite book, the Book of Job, the devil's complaint to God (in chapter two) was that God had unfairly blessed and prospered Job. The devil has more wisdom sometimes than Christians. He realizes that God is the one who blesses. Don't be afraid of the truth. Don't ever be afraid to challenge your own theology, and don't be afraid to challenge the theology of others concerning this area—provided you have the maturity to do so in love. Please don't misunderstand what I am teaching. I am not espousing the notion of pushing God around. That is utter silliness. We can place a demand on what God has said in His Word, but we do *not* place demands on God. We draw on the faithfulness of God to perform His Word. We place a demand on the circumstances and situations to line up with what God has said.

Neither am I espousing egotism; rather, this is a position of humility, because only a humble person can accept the word of another. An egotist accepts the word of no one who disagrees with him. In the first seven verses of Luke 5, Peter and his crew had been out fishing all night, and they had caught absolutely *nothing*. They came back ashore and began the routine of mending their nets when Jesus came on the scene. He said to Peter, "I want to use your boat. Row out a little way." So Peter rowed out while Jesus taught. When He finished, He dismissed the people and told Peter, "Okay, now row out to the deep and drop your nets on that side of the boat."

Now, anyone who knows anything at all about fishing knows that the best time to catch fish is either early in the morning or late in the afternoon. Those are the times when the fish school and feed. You can also

catch fish at night if you have a light because they're attracted to light. But fishermen generally embark on their quests either
early in the morning or late in the afternoon.
In Luke 5, Peter had come in after having
been out all night long and catching nothing. Then Jesus, a carpenter, came along
and made a seemingly outrageous request.
How did Peter respond? He said, "Lord,
we have toiled all night and caught nothing."

"NEVERTHELESS, AT THY WORD"

Between the lines you can almost read,
"You're the preacher, but I'm a fisherman.
This is my business." He said, "Lord, we
have toiled all night and caught nothing."
But he didn't stop there. He said, "Never-
theless...."

I can just imagine Jesus' concern, because
the last time He had heard "nevertheless"
was in Exodus when God sent the twelve
to spy out Canaan. They came back and
said, "It's everything God said, and here is
proof of it. *Nevertheless* there be giants in

the land and we are as grasshoppers in our own sight." "Nevertheless" meant disobedience. But this time, Peter is saying, "We've toiled all night and taken nothing, *nevertheless* at Your Word...." There was no logical reason to honor Jesus' request. Nevertheless, Peter did as He asked. He acted upon the Word. What happened? He let down the net and proceeded to catch such a multitude of fishes that his net began to break. He had to call his partners to come out and help with his boat. They got out there with Peter, started hauling it in, and the catch was so great that both boats began to sink. This was all because Peter said, "Nevertheless at Thy Word." Why did he make this statement of faith? Because he recognized the command, he recognized the power inherent in the command, and he obeyed. That's what faith does. Faith simply obeys the command.

They said, "Lord increase our faith."

Jesus answered, "Use what you have." Recognize that faith is your servant, a tool given to you to be used, not to be put on a shelf.

Let's look again at Luke 17, starting at verse 11.

> And it came to pass, as he went to Jerusalem, that he passed through the midst of Samaria and Galilee. And as he entered into a certain village, there met him ten men that were lepers, which stood afar off: And they lifted up their voices, and said, Jesus, Master, have mercy on us.

Notice that the lepers came for cleansing. Ten of them, standing afar off, pleading, "Jesus, have mercy on us." What does Jesus do in response? "And when he saw them," verse 14, "He *said*...." He issued a command. He spoke. And in the words that He spoke there was inherent power to carry out what was said. All it needed was faith on the part of the hearer to be mixed with it in order to produce the result. "And when he saw them, he said unto them, Go shew yourselves unto the priests...." Why did He say that? These men were full of leprosy, and His response to their plea was to send them to the priests. But there is something deeper here. God provided healing for the leper under the Levitical law, and when he was healed, the leper was to show himself to the priest and offer a certain sacrifice. Now look at it again: "Go show yourselves to the priest." He didn't say, "Be healed." He said, "Go show yourselves to the priest." In other words, He told them to act upon what had already been provided. "And it came to pass, that, as they went, they were cleansed" (Luke 17:14). As they left, the healing power of God came into operation because they obeyed the command that had been given. Why? They were exercising their faith; they were *doing* something. They weren't maintaining the status quo, or trying to talk themselves out of believing that their day had come. They were doing something with what had been said.

FAITH, NOT FEELING

Most of us would have waited until we were cleansed before we went. We want to know *now*, before we go and make fools of ourselves. But we need to *do* before we *feel*. Faith does before it feels.

If I *feel* healed in my body, I don't need to *believe*. "By Christ's stripes I am healed." It's obvious—my health is here and now. Faith speaks of things that are not as though they already were. A lot of us are like the lepers of Jesus' day in that we don't think we deserve to be healed. In those days, whenever a leper went out in public, they'd have to cry, "Leper, unclean!" and stay away from everybody. They'd have to announce themselves in advance, and people would scatter away from them. Psychologically, their conditions must have been magnified tremendously by the reactions of others to the point where any self-esteem was impossible. After a while, they probably felt that they deserved this rejection, and that they certainly didn't deserve to be healed.

That is where some of us are today. The truth of the matter is that none of us deserve to be healed. If you study Romans 4, you'll find out that God cannot give you what you deserve. God gives you what you don't deserve because it comes by grace through faith. What God gives you must be of grace so it can be received by faith. We can't earn it. Earning and receiving by faith are mutually exclusive concepts. You will never be righteous enough to deserve healing. It is a gift from God.

The challenge is to learn to receive by faith. When you've honestly, genuinely, really received something, you have no trouble believing that it belongs to you. Consequently, you'll act like it belongs to you. When you've understood this, you've understood faith. The ten lepers didn't earn healing. They didn't fall down and worship Him, they didn't confess Him as Lord, they didn't repent, they didn't do anything. They said, "Have mercy"—and He did. But it goes even further. Verse 15: "And one of them, when he saw that he was healed, turned back, and with a loud voice glorified God." Leprosy was the AIDS of its day, and the stigma attached to the disease was probably worse. When you had leprosy, parts of your body rotted away before your eyes. Some of these ten lepers probably had fingers, toes, parts of their ears and noses missing.

From this cruel disease they were delivered, but those body parts were still missing. One of the ten, after he got what he didn't deserve, recognized that he was healed, and with a loud voice began to glorify God.

Luke 17:16-19: "And fell down on his face at his feet, giving him thanks: and he was a Samaritan." A Samaritan had no claim to healing at all under the Mosaic Law.

Verse 17:

> And Jesus answering said, Were there not ten cleansed? but where are the nine? There are not found that returned to give glory to God, save this stranger. And he said unto him, Arise, go thy way: thy faith has made thee whole.

Not only did this fellow get cleansed, but he was made whole. Understand the difference between being cleansed and being made whole. Being cleansed is getting healed. The leprosy was gone. But when he came back and glorified God, everything that had been missing was restored!

In light of this example, I want to always

be sure to be one who comes back and glorifies God. I don't just want to be healed, I want complete restoration!

When I first started learning this truth, it sounded strange to me because I was so concerned about having my needs met. I couldn't figure out how God wanted to meet my need more than I wanted my need met. But the way He wanted to meet my need was by dispatching me to meet somebody else's need. That sounded foreign to me until I began to do it. All of a sudden I found out that as I busied myself with the needs of others, mine were met without my asking. I quit being self-centered and became Christ-centered. When you become Christ-centered, you automatically become people-centered. If you call yourself a Christian, a lover of God, that is exactly where you need to be.

3

The Law of Faith vs. The Law of Works

BELIEVING IS SEEING

We have learned previously that faith is not blind; faith, in fact, is the means by which we can see clearly. Second Corinthians 4:18 says to look not at the things that are seen, but rather to the things that are not seen, because the things that are seen are temporal, temporary, and subject to change. But things which are not seen are eternal.

The Word of God, therefore, tells me to focus my attention on what I cannot see. Keep your eyes on the answer, not the problem. Does that mean to suggest that we should ignore the problem? You see, if I don't recognize the problem, I can't find the answer. You cannot find a specific answer without a clear understanding of the problem.

As always, there is a balance that needs to be maintained if we are to understand the Scriptures. We are to focus on the spiritual for no reason other than the fact that it is in the Spiritual realm that solutions may be found. Situations and circumstances change; the Word of God is eternal, living, powerful and capable of changing situations and circumstances. Therefore, we look not at what can be seen with our natural eyes, but at what cannot be tangibly seen.

If I am in a place of financial adversity, I don't look at the financial adversity. I look at the prosperity God has promised to me. Why? Because that's what I don't see. If I have a million dollars in my checkbook, it's not a problem to go out and buy things. But when I have ten dollars in my checkbook, and I need a million dollars, the answer lies in the spiritual realm. Once it comes into fruition, then we don't need to use faith for it anymore. Faith is for those things that we don't see. "Now, faith is the substance of things hoped for, the evidence of things not seen." (Heb. 11:1). Your faith is the substance and the evidence of what you're believing for before it manifests itself. We must exercise our faith before we can see it in the natural. That means I've got to see it in the realm of the spirit—through the eye of faith. *Faith sees clearly.* It looks not at what is seen in the natural, but at what God has said. Faith takes hold of what God has promised and refuses to relent until what God has promised comes to fruition in your life. True faith is determined and tenacious.

There are many times when we are tempted to give up. The enemy is always attempting to get us to give up, because the minute you do, you become non-productive. You become just another pew-sitter in the church. You're going to heaven, but not doing any damage to the devil's kingdom. He couldn't keep you from getting born-again, or from getting filled with the Spirit, but he wants to keep you from getting healed.

What we need to realize is that the devil can no more keep you from getting healed than he could keep you from getting saved. If he could have stopped you from doing anything that God said you could do, he would have stopped you in the beginning. Before you were saved, the devil tried to keep you from going to church. When you got to the church, he tried to convince you that it was all nonsense. When you responded to the altar call, he told you that it was your emotions; he suggested that it would go away once you came to your senses. When you got filled with the Holy Spirit, he told you that it was gibberish and it meant nothing. *You are where you are because you responded to all the devil's lies with faith.* How did you know that you were really born-again when the devil told you you weren't? What was your proof? How did you know you were really baptized in the Holy Spirit? You knew because you had faith in what God said.

You might say, "But, Brother Mike, I had the inner witness." That's wonderful, but that's not proof. That notion goes by the wayside the first time you wake up not feeling saved.

Romans 10:9 says that if you confess with your mouth and believe in your heart that God raised Jesus from the dead, you are saved—whether you feel like it or not. That is how you knew. God's promise to you was the proof of your salvation.

How do I know I'm filled with the spirit and speak in other tongues? Luke 11:11, 13 says:

> If a son shall ask bread of any of you that is a father, will he give him a stone? or if he ask a fish, will he for a fish give him a serpent?... If ye then, being evil, know how to give good gifts unto your children: how much more shall your heavenly Father give the Holy Spirit to them that ask him?

That's how I know. I also know because my mind does not comprehend it. What's more, I didn't learn it. So if I don't understand it, and it isn't something I've learned, the odds are pretty good that I'm speaking in other tongues, because the Word of God says (in 1 Corinthians 14:14) that when I pray in another tongue my spirit prays, but my understanding is unfruitful.

THE LAW OF FAITH IS SIMPLE

The law of faith is very simple. Believe what God says, act like it's so, and *He* will bring it to pass. For some strange reason, most of us want to earn what we get.

> But now the righteousness of God without the law is manifested, being witnessed by the law and the prophets; Even the righteousness of God which is by faith of Jesus Christ unto all and upon all them that believe: for there is no difference: For all have sinned, and come short of the glory of God; Being justified freely by his grace through the redemption that is in Christ Jesus: Whom God hath set forth to be a propitiation through faith in his blood, to declare

his righteousness for the remission of sins that are past, through the forbearance of God.... Where is boasting then? It is excluded. By what law? of works? Nay: but by the law of faith. Therefore we conclude that a man is justified by faith without the deeds of the law (Romans 3:21-25, 27-28).

The righteousness of God was manifested outside of the Law. It was not manifested through the Law, but outside of it. It was attested to by the Law, and by all the prophets. They were pointing to the righteousness of God because God was positioning His people so that He could bless them. While the love of God is unconditional, His promises are contingent upon our being in right standing with Him.

Our success in handling circumstances with which we strive and battle—whether they be in the form of sickness, inadequate finances, mental or emotional problems, or problems in relationships—depends upon getting to the place where we need to be with God. Strip everything away, and what you're left with is the fundamental premise of faith: if I believe I'm right with God, I'll have no problem believing that God will give me what I ask for.

We can all remember times when we prayed and studied enough, were all worked up to believe God, just *knew* that it would come to pass, and, sure enough, it did. So we strive to get back to feeling the way we did then, because that, apparently, was the formula that worked. So we spend all our time striving to obtain something that's already been given to us, and the devil just keeps us going around in circles. He deceives us into looking at the things that are seen, and He keeps throwing things our way that will keep us from feeling how we need to feel in order for us to believe that we're right with God. We try to work our way there, rather than letting God give us things. While there is such a thing as the fruits of our labor, it is not to be confused with faith.

If I am the best employee on the job, do more work than anybody else, and get a raise; I *earned* that raise. That raise came as a result of works. Now I am certainly not suggesting that we should all goof off at work and believe God for a raise. Diligence is a godly attribute. My point is that we need to understand the difference between faith and works. Works certainly have their reward; but faith will get you what no amount of work ever can. We need to do all that we have in our power to do, but faith ensures that what we do will always be enough.

Romans 3:27 points out, "Where is boasting then? It is excluded. By what law? of works? Nay: but by the law of faith." This portion of Scripture is significant for what we're trying to establish here. You see, under the Old Covenant, I would have to bring in my sacrifice to have my sin covered. It was never *dealt with*—it was simply covered. And if I did all the right things as prescribed by the Law, then I could have my sins covered. The problem was that you had to do those things in faith in the first place for them to work. Yet most of the Jews were doing them ritualistically simply because those were the rules.

Too many times, things that start off in faith wind up in the flesh. Paul spoke to the Galatians about that. In fact, that's a constantly recurring theme in the writings of Paul— the concept of the difference between faith and works. Notice verse 28 of Romans 3: "Therefore we conclude that a man is justified by faith without the deeds of the law." An individual is justified by faith outside of the deeds of the law. This verse doesn't leave much room for debate.

However, we are confronted with a seeming paradox when we consider James 2:20: "But wilt thou know, O vain man, that faith without works is dead?" How do you reconcile the two? I'm justified by faith without the deeds of the Law, but yet faith without works is dead.

Paul did not say that we are justified by faith without corresponding actions. He said we're justified by faith. So if James says "faith without works is dead," I'm justified by faith with its corresponding actions. We cannot perform in order to attain justification; we perform our faith. We work *from salvation* as we exercise and strengthen our faith; we do not work towards it. It's a completely different kind of motivation behind our actions.

Most Christians are doing things to become something. We don't receive because we're doing something to become something we already are. If I do this, this and that, then I will earn the blessings of God. We don't think of it in those terms, but that is exactly what we tend to do. There will always be people who would go to the altar for healing, have the preacher pray for them, but they don't see any manifestation. They will go home and pray, "God, I'm going to show you I have faith. I'm throwing my medicine away." That's not faith. That is stupidity. Faith is not inclined to prove anything. If I'm healed, I don't need the medicine. But if I have not received the manifestation, I need it.

Others get to the place where they think God is withholding because their life is less than perfect. If that's you, you'll never get anything in the way of answered prayer because your life will never be perfect until you get to heaven. Only then will your mortality put on immortality. We can grow and mature in the knowledge of God through fellowship with Him in prayer and study of His Word. But if you think you need to have it all together before God moves, you're wasting time.

THE BLOOD OF JESUS

Thank God for the Blood. Your belief in God is imputed to you as righteousness. When you've missed it, you can pray, and God is faithful and just to forgive your sins (1 John 1:9). Once you've done that, the slate is clean. You don't need to start at square one again. You don't have to go back to the beginning and start all over. Faith says, "I'm righteous, I have right standing with God. Therefore, in the name of Jesus I believe that I receive God's provision for my need." It is not because of what I can do. No one can earn the blessing of God. But through faith, anyone can have it. That's the point. That's why Jesus died.

For what saith the scripture? Abraham believed God, and it was counted unto him for righteousness. Now to him that worketh is the reward not reckoned of grace, but of debt. But to him that worketh not, but believeth on him that justifieth the ungodly, his faith is counted for righteousness.... Cometh this blessedness then upon the circumcision only, or upon the uncircumcision also? for we say that faith was reckoned to Abraham for righteousness (Rom. 4:3-5, 9).

For the law having a shadow of good things to come, and not the very image of the things, can never with those sacrifices which they offered year by year continually made the comers thereunto perfect (Heb. 10:1).

In these Scriptures, Paul draws a distinct contrast between faith and the Law. The Law, Paul says, is a *shadow* of good things to come, but not the substance, which is Christ. The Law is the perfect standard that reflects the iniquity of us all. Have you ever noticed that the law never goes into effect until you break it? Have you ever driven on the highway between fifty and fifty-five miles per hour, and started wondering about where the police were? Then, when you hit sixty and sixty-five, you really begin to look for the "cherry-tops." What happened? Your consciousness of the law became much greater when you broke it.

All the Law can do is to show you what you can't do. It keeps you under guilt and condemnation; it reflects something good.

In the Old Testament, you see an understanding of the law of faith. After he had committed adultery with Bathsheba, and after he had Uriah killed, King David still called on God for mercy to forgive him for what he knew was not lawful to be forgiven of. Under the Law, the penalty for adultery was death, just as it was for premeditated murder. There was no sacrifice that he could offer to enable him to be forgiven.

Yet David cried out for mercy, and God forgave him because David understood that the Law was a type and shadow. He went beyond the Law, to the Lawgiver. He understood the nature and character of his God.

Here, too, there is a balance to be maintained. We need to exert control over our actions. We need to constantly renew our minds.

> Do not be conformed to this world— this age, fashioned after and adapted to its external, superficial customs. But be transformed [changed] by the [entire] renewal of your mind— by its new ideals and its new attitude... (Rom. 12:2 TAB).

So how can I have a new standard if I don't set that standard before me? The standard to which we aspire is the Word of God. I am the righteousness of God in Christ Jesus. Therefore, because God said that I am righteousness, I can find out what righteousness SAYS and what it DOES. And as I live in Christ and learn from His

Word, that standard becomes increasingly clear in its applications to every-day life. As the clarity of that standard becomes greater, conformity to it becomes more ingrained in my patterns of thought and action because I begin to graduate from faith to faith (Rom. 1:17). We must become more God-conscious rather than more conscious of the world's standards. Let's revisit Romans 4 at some length, starting with verse 12:

> And the father of circumcision to them who are not of the circumcision only, but who also walk in the steps of that faith of our father Abraham, which he had being yet uncircumcised. For the promise, that he should be the heir of the world, was not to Abraham, or to his seed, through the law, but through the righteousness of faith. For if they which are of the law be heirs, faith is made void, and the promise made of none effect: Because the law worketh wrath: for where no law is, there is no transgression.

Notice three things. First, Paul says in verse 13 that the promise was given to Abraham, not through the Law, but through "the righteousness of faith." Secondly, in verse 14 he says that righteousness through the Law is impossible if for no other reason than because it would render faith a void and unnecessary concept. The third point is found in verse 15. If there is no transgression where there is no law, then only where there is law can transgression exist.

Read the next few verses out of the Amplified version closely.

> Therefore [inheriting] the promise is the outcome of faith and depends [entirely] on faith, in order that it might be given as an act of grace (unmerited favor), to make it stable and valid and guaranteed to all his descendants; not only to the devotees and adherents of the Law but also to those who share the faith of Abraham, who is [thus] the father of us all, As it is written, I have made you the father of many nations —

He was appointed our father— in the sight of God in Whom he believed, who gives life to the dead and speaks of the nonexistent things that [He has foretold and promised] as if they already existed.... He did not weaken in faith when he considered the [utter] impotence of his own body, which was as good as dead because he was a hundred years old, or [when he considered] the barrenness of (Sarah's deadened) womb. No unbelief of distrust made him waver or doubtingly question concerning the promise of God, but he grew strong and was empowered by faith as he gave praise and glory to God, Fully satisfied and assured that God was able and mighty to keep His word and to do what he had promised (Rom. 4: 16-17, 19-21 TAB).

I can envision God waiting for us to run our course until we get to the end of ourselves, and only then realize that God was waiting for us to come to Him from the very beginning. God says, *I know all about it. Here*

I am, ready to perform what I've promised.

If we'd just learn to quit trying and let God perform, it would work. We need to walk in it. Allow God to be God. We need to believe what God said, act like it's true and leave Him to perform it. Leave the "how" of it to Him.

You'll never regret it.

4

Obedience to His Commands

Without realizing it, we've lived by faith all of our lives in the natural realm. You're probably sitting in a chair as you read this. How did you know that the chair would hold you up? You had a natural faith. You saw the construction of the chair, you knew the chair was designed to hold you up, you assumed it would and you sat down.

We don't need to be engineers before we can sit in a chair, but the point is that these little assumptions we make are a part of everyone's life. As human beings, we are used to operating in faith.

How do you know that when you turn

the key in the ignition of your car that it is going to start up? Because yours is a natural faith. When you turn your stove on, when you turn your lights on and all the rest, you're living and moving in a realm of natural faith in the things that you have come to rely on. We never wonder if a chair will hold us up before we sit in it, and we never expect the light switch to fail. We need to transfer that same type of trust to the Word of God. When it comes to the Word of God, it's amazing how we trust it, *but....* It works, *however....* It happened that way once, but what about this time? We have trust and confidence in natural things, but yet in that which is more real than the natural, which is the realm of the Spirit of God, we lack that same trust and confidence. God will provide the finances I need, but I had better get a second mortgage on my house just in case. I believe God will heal me, but I had better run down to the doctor anyway. I am not advocating that we refrain from visiting doctors, but that we trust God and His Word first in all that we do.

It is good for us to be in situations where we can't do anything for ourselves, because when we are weak, then He is strong. As long as there is something left to do, we do it.

In previous chapters, we learned that what we receive as the result of works is owed to us and is to be considered wages, not the gift of God. If I can earn it, God doesn't send forth the Holy Spirit, and allow Him to pray through us with "groanings that cannot be uttered" in travailing prayer, that God might bring to birth His purposes in the closing hours of time.

Let's forget our past failings and through faith look beyond the Red Sea, look past the lions' mouths, turn from Lazarus' tomb to the Son of God, and look to Him to give us our hearts' desires "...for with God nothing shall be impossible (Matt. 19:26).

My bet is that ninety-nine percent of us misdiagnose the situation and wonder where we've missed it. Our misperception causes Satan to work undetected, without confrontation. We are so sin-conscious, conscious of our frailties and shortcomings, that the minute anything negative comes, we try to find out why it happened instead of standing against the devil.

Don't ever waste your time with "why?" In case you haven't found out yet, we live in an imperfect world. The battle is joined. Fight it and win. And if you must, you can then investigate "why?"

God has given us an umbrella. But even when you have a good umbrella, your feet can get sopping wet. Regardless of the size or quality of the umbrella, we must still walk through the slop.

Jesus says, "He that is washed needeth not save to wash his feet, but is clean every whit..." (John 13:10). Why did He say that our feet should be washed? Because we walk in a dirty world. There are certain realities that we're going to have deal with because of the world we live in. We are not of the world, but we sure are in it. And because we're in the world, we must deal with what the world brings our way.

We have to change our perspectives. We must change our view of ourselves and begin to understand that when we're dealing with matters of faith, what I earn and deserve God can never give to me. I can never do enough to earn anything from God.

Everything God gives me is by grace, and it is received by faith. I do what I do for the Lord as a function of what I am. I'm not trying to *become*.

THE FAITH ATTITUDE

The same attitude carries over even into our ideas of faith itself. Some people feel the need to "do" in an effort to live by faith. People give all their money away to prove their faith, when all they've done is demonstrate their utter ignorance of the Word of God. Under the pretense of faith, here again you have an example of trying to earn something from God.

> And being not weak in faith, he considered not his own body now dead, when he was about an hundred years old, neither yet the deadness of Sarah's womb: He staggered not at the promise of God through unbelief; but was strong in faith, giving glory to God; And being fully persuaded that, what he had promised, he was able also to perform (Rom. 4:19-21).

He was fully persuaded, completely convinced in his mind, without any doubt, that what God had promised, He was able to perform. Abraham was as sure that God would honor His Word as you are when you sit in your favorite chair that it will hold you up. You can get to the place where you don't even think about it anymore. You just expect it to be, and you act as if it already is.

Years ago, I was making $25.00 a week while I was on the staff of a church. I was going to college full-time also. It was great for 1972. I felt I was in tall cotton! My wife, Martha, finally got a job and began making $80.00 a week. So between the two of us, we were doing great. It amazed me then, however, and it has never ceased to amaze me since, how bills grow on the same scale as your pay! No matter how much you have, you always have bills! Back then, even going out to eat at Denny's was a matter of faith. Martha and I would ask ourselves, "What would we do if we had the money?" We would go out! So we went out— to Denny's. The point is, that in our own small way, we began to count on God's faithfulness

to His Word in our lives. We didn't do anything stupid or exaggerated that would get
us into trouble.

The life of faith is a growing process. We
need to take care to be wise and faithful
stewards of what God has given us *now*.
But we also need to realize that it's the little steps we take along the way that will
prepare us eventually for the big leap. The
little things that we do, day by day, are
what build confidence in God.

Take the following principle as a rule of
thumb— if people cannot trust your word,
the odds are that you'll have trouble trusting God's Word. Like it or not, we tend to
project our attitudes and behavior on others, including God.

If you think nothing of going back on
your word and reneging on your promises,
you probably believe that God behaves the
same way. Women especially, for instance,
are affected deeply in their relationships
with God as a result of their relationships
with their natural fathers. This is a strange
but true phenomenon that should motivate
us in our interpersonal relationships.

In Luke 17:6, we read: "...Be thou plucked up by the root, and be thou planted in the sea; *and it should obey you.*" The Living Bible reads, "And your command would bring immediate results" (Luke 17:6, TLB). Note the word "command." A command is a demand that has been placed or brought into existence by the use of words.

Jesus said, "Doth he thank the servant because he does the things that were commanded him..." (Luke 17:9). Notice that it says "commanded him." God issues commands.

In Numbers 23, Balaam tried to curse the nation of Israel, and the only thing that came out of his mouth were blessings. King Balak, who commissioned him to curse Israel, complained.

> And he took up his parable, and said, Rise up, Balak, and hear; hearken unto me, thou son of Zippor: God is not a man, that he should lie; neither the son of man, that he should repent: hath he said, and shall he not do it? or hath he spoken,

and shall he not make it good? Behold, I have received commandment to bless: and he hath blessed; and I cannot reverse it (Num. 23:18-20).

God has blessed, and He has never stopped blessing His people. Balaam went on to instruct Balak on how to sabotage God's blessings. He told Balak to send women in amongst the Israelites in order to intermarry so as to subvert the purity of their religion, introduce them to foreign gods and all the rest. Only then could a curse stick to the Israelites.

But pronouncing a curse upon Israel is futile, *because no one other than the people themselves could do anything to reverse God's blessing.* Balaam's alternate plan is one that the devil has used with great success. God has blessed us, and no one can reverse the blessing. So what does Satan do? He tries to come in and subvert. He tries to plant things in our lives that will cause us to abandon our faith. But God has blessed, and the only one who can change that is you.

In *Vine's Expository Dictionary of New Testament Words we* read as follows. "I [Jesus] am the one whose will and whose commands must be obeyed, both in heaven and earth, therefore you go" (Matt. 28:18). That tells me that if He is the one whose will and whose commands must be obeyed, both in heaven and in earth, then if I speak what He's commanded, it must be obeyed. This is true because Jesus is the only person in history to rise from the dead so that He could become the executor of His own will (Heb. 9:16-17)! His will *must* be obeyed.

The devil has used every weapon he has to keep this from coming to pass, including murdering Jesus. But Jesus went to the very pit of hell and rose from the dead not only to issue the command, but to be alive to enforce it!

The Church needs to be more militant in prayer. We've lacked confidence in our prayer lives because of a lack of faith. We've been kind of hoping that God would do it. But what most people don't know is that the biblical word for "hope" in the original language means *confident, favorable expectation*.

Most of us are *wishing* when we think we're hoping. Your prayers will yield results once you learn to be confident in what God has declared. If I have confidence in what He said, He will do what He said in my life. He must, because it's not my reputation that's at stake, but His. God is not a man that He should lie.

> And it shall come to pass, if thou shalt hearken diligently to the voice of the Lord thy God, to observe and to do all his commandments which I command thee this day, that the Lord thy God will set thee on high above all nations of the earth: And all these blessings shall come on thee, and overtake thee, if thou shalt hearken unto the voice of the Lord thy God (Deut. 28:1-2).
> This book of the law shall not depart out of thy mouth; but thou shalt meditate therein day and night, that thou mayest observe to do according to all that is written therein: for then thou shalt make thy way prosperous,

and then thou shalt have good success (Jos. 1:8).

God's voice is God's Word. So if I'm going to hearken diligently to the voice of the Lord my God, that means I'm going to have to hearken diligently to the Word. But why must I hearken diligently to the Word? I hearken to the Word to *observe to do*. I don't just read the Word to get fed, or just for the sake of reading it, but so I can do it. Many observe, but not many observe to do.

Ephesians 6 tell us to put on the whole armor of God, so we can stand against the wiles of the devil. A lot of us put on our armor, but we never stand. We put on the armor to do battle.

Some have thought that getting saved and getting filled with the Holy Spirit was their ticket to peace and prosperity, an insurance that nothing will ever go wrong. But while peace and prosperity are certainly among our entitlements as Christians, we must also get comfortable with the idea that the world will bring tribulation.

Whosoever believeth that Jesus is the Christ is born of God: and every one that loveth him that begat loveth him also that is begotten of him. By this we know that we love the children of God, when we love God, and keep his commandments. For this is the love of God, that we keep his commandments: and his commandments are not grievous. For whatsoever is born of God overcometh the world: and this is the victory that overcometh the world, even our faith (I John 5:1- 4).

The faith that overcomes the world works by love, as shown above and in Galatians 5:6. Faith is energized by love, and love is demonstrated by our obedience to God's commandments. I love my wife, but I must do things to demonstrate that to her. The intent is not to prove to her, but to perform my love for her. If I love her, I will do things; just as if I love God, there must be corresponding action. We keep the demands that are placed upon us by words.

Jesus boiled all the commandments in Matthew 22 down to two: love God, and love people. To love, in essence, is our only command. Our love for God and for others will steer us into the direction God wants for us. This, in turn, activates faith because our faith becomes a function of our relationship with God. Our love for God will produce a relationship with Him that will build our confidence in the Person of God, the Father, not simply in words on a page or from a preacher. You know your "Daddy," and you know personally that He cannot fail to perform His Word. Your faith in Him is a by-product of your love for Him—your appreciation and gratitude for what He's done for you, what He's brought you out of and what He's doing through you.

Your love for God will constrain you to walk only in what pleases God. And if you find yourself doing the wrong things, that means you need to spend more time with the One you love, and refresh yourself in that.

It's like in a marriage relationship. Your

love for your spouse is red-hot at times, and ice-cold at others. But in the times when it seems to be ice-cold, that's not the time to bail out, because marriage is based on commitment, on a relationship and a covenant: not based on feelings.

If you stick with the covenant long enough and place a demand on what God has said, the feelings will come. When you start to get cold, that's when you know you need to spend more time with Daddy, more time in the Word. It's time to turn the television off and put on a tape.

We need to have consistent doses of God's Word. Years ago, I had asthma that was so bad that I had to be medically discharged from the army. I was getting shots twice a week, and I had an inhaler that I carried around in my back pocket, and I had pills that were so large they looked like pills you would give to horses. I didn't go any place without my inhaler. When I went swimming, it was in the pocket of my swimming trunks.

GET A HOLD ON THE WORD

Then I started getting a hold on the Word, however, and began to stand against the asthma, or so I thought. One day, Martha and I went to a Kenneth Copeland meeting in Burbank, California along with some friends of ours. I chose not to bring my inhaler with me to the meeting. I decided to take a step of faith. I did, however, bring one of the "horse pills" with me.

During the meeting, it got harder and harder for me to breathe. The more Brother Cope-land preached, the harder it got for me to breathe.

We were supposed to go to our friend's house afterwards, so I slipped into the restroom and popped that "horse pill." It was supposed to work within about a half an hour, but an hour later, while we were still in the meeting, it wasn't working. We went to our friend's house, and three or four hours later the pill still hadn't done its work!

When we finally got home, anyone standing between me and the inhaler was in some serious danger. In a couple of days, I went to my regularly scheduled doctor's appointment for a shot. I said to him, "This stuff is not working."

He replied, "What do you mean?"

"Well, I took that pill and it didn't work."

He asked, "Have you been taking one every six hours?"

"No."

"You don't understand. You must take one every six hours and constantly have that medication in your body so that when you are really having trouble, you can take another pill and the added dosage will relieve your discomfort."

My response was, "There is no way I'm going to fill my body with a form of speed every six hours of every day of my life, and extra when I need it. I was delivered from drugs. No way will I go into a lifestyle of drug dependency." Something had clicked inside of me and it got me mad enough to fight! I decided then and there that I was never taking one of those pills again.

The principle is that instead of having a steady dosage of drugs in my body to whip the asthma, I maintained steady dosages of the Word of God in me. And when I was in particular discomfort, instead of taking more drugs, I hunkered down on the Word a little more than usual.

We need to keep the Word of God constantly within us, so that when adversity comes, we can add to the reserve we already have. The problem with some of us, however, is that when adversity strikes, instead of taking an extra dose of the Word, we find ourselves starting from scratch.

The Victory that Overcomes the World

The victory that overcomes the world is our faith, and our faith works by love. The love of God constrains me. I know that I love God because I keep His commandments, and I do that which He said. I keep the demands that are placed on me by words. And if I keep the demands that are placed on me by words, if I hearken diligently to the voice of the Lord my God to observe to do, then all these blessings shall come on me and overtake me. But I must observe to do the demands that are placed upon me by words.

If God gives me a commandment and I do it, then I can issue a command based on what He said, and I can expect it to be done. But if God gives me a commandment and I don't do it, when I turn around and issue a command based on His Word, I'm not going to have confidence that it will happen, because I'm not under authority. And if I'm not under authority, I can't operate in authority. As I receive the command, as I observe to do, then I command. Why? Because I'm under authority. What He says, I do.

Have you ever noticed that people who understand authority never have a problem exercising authority? It's the people who are tired of being under authority who have problems with it.

Someone who understands authority doesn't lord it over someone because they themselves are submitted to somebody else. They do what their boss tells them, so they figure you'll do what they tell you. And they stay in that position because they obey those that are over them.

Jesus said, "...ye shall ask what you will and it shall be done unto you" (John 15:7). The word "ask" means to literally make a demand for something that is due.

God told us to make a demand for the things that are due to us. They're not due to you, however, unless you are assuming your proper position in God. When you are, what you ask in prayer becomes your entitlement.

"Thou shalt decree a thing and it shall be established unto thee," (Job 22:28). A decree is an order that has the force of law behind it. It is a command for something to be. If I decree a thing and it shall be established, that then tells me that if I don't decree, nothing shall be established. "Where the word of a king is, there is power: and who may say unto him, What doest thou?" (Eccles. 8:4). You don't ask a king, "What do you think you're doing?" Where his word is, there is power. In Job 22:28, we read, "...and the light shall shine upon thy ways." I will never have the light to be able to do until I make the decree. You'll decree a thing, it will be established and then light will shine on your path. When I see nothing, I make the decree. And when I make the decree, it is established as far as God is concerned. Then once it's established, light comes to show me how to walk in it.

We've got to get back to being militant believers. We've got to get back to believing that what God said is true, acting like it's so and using our faith to command, demand and refuse to put up with things.

When we lived in California, we had a family of skunks that decided to take up residence underneath our house. I was getting ready to let our dog out one night, and I turned the light on to find one of these creatures in the middle of our back yard.

I knew that if I let my dog out, it would chase that skunk. I screamed out the window, "I have dominion and authority over *all* that's upon the earth. So, you foul smelling skunk, get off my property, in the name of Jesus. You obey me, and leave and I erase all traces of you!" A minute later, the skunk was gone and I was able to let my dog out. Normally, the scent from a skunk lingers and the dog goes crazy trying to find the skunk. This skunk, however, did not leave even a trace. I exercised my authority over that skunk by the Word of God. Before long, the entire skunk family had gone.

We must get to the place where we make demands and decrees because we know we are under authority, because we obey what God says. Therefore, we know what we say will come to pass. It's not because we're trying to be somebody, but because of who we already are.

5

Hearing Isn't Enough

Many of us go a certain distance by faith, but then we forget what brought us to the present points in our lives. We get weary in well doing. The Bible tells us that if we do not grow weary, and if we don't faint, eventually we will reap. But many fall short in this, and when we do, we forfeit the benefits we would have had if we had persevered in faith.

WHAT GOD HAS DONE

I want to be able to do increasingly more for God all the time, but I know I can't do increasingly more for God unless I learn to operate in faith. The things we're able to do through faith never cease to amaze me. At the end of each year I sit back and take stock of the things that happened over that year, and I think, "Praise God! But how in the world are we going to be able to do more in the coming year than we did last year?" I look at it this way every single year.

I remember when I first started to travel overseas. For years I wanted to travel. Eventually I got as far as Mexico. (That's not saying a whole lot, because I lived in Southern California at the time!) All one had to do was to drive three hours to get to Mexico.

In 1981 I traveled out of the country once. In 1982 I traveled out of the country twice. I thought it was wonderful. Since that time, I've been out of the U.S. so often that it seems almost ridiculous in retrospect. Sometimes I wonder if I should establish a separate residence in London, in Norway or in Poland.

It thrills me to see what God has done in the establishment of our World Outreach Bible Schools. Just recently, for example, we've opened three Bible schools in Brazil. A few months after opening those training schools, we opened additional Bible schools in Argentina. Ghana, Nigeria and Singapore are all on the slate for future development. The requests to establish schools on a worldwide basis keep me busier than I ever imagined.

With the budget I operate with, it's impossible to do all the things I do. If you looked at the numbers, you'd know that God takes care of me. That's called operating in faith—not in presumption, but by *faith*.

The Apostle Peter, after he gave the people of God a tongue-lashing, began to encourage them in their faith; he exhorted them to develop the type of life-style they were supposed to live. He said, "But of course, you're already established in this present truth, but I'm just saying it by way of a reminder." We all need reminders from time to time.

Let's look at Luke 17, beginning at verse 5, where the apostles came to Jesus. They had been with Him for a period of time and they had witnessed the miracles, the signs and wonders. They knew what had transpired. They had personally experienced the power of God.

Jesus had said to them, "Behold, I give unto you power to tread on serpents and scorpions, and over all the power of the enemy, and nothing shall by any means harm you." They liked these words. Now they came to Jesus and asked, "Increase our faith" (Luke 17:5).

Notice that the Scriptures don't say that He laid hands on them. Faith is not imparted by the laying on of hands. You cannot receive faith in the prayer line either, but you can have the power of God ministered to you. The gift that's on the inside of you can be stirred up, but we can't lay hands on you and give you faith. Romans 10:17 says that "...faith cometh by hearing" —and hearing, and hearing, and hearing....

But what is faith? If I believe in my heart and confess with my mouth, that's faith. Faith is the substance of things hoped for, the evidence of things not seen—and on and on the description goes.

There is a very simple definition of faith, however, that helps us to understand the intent of the Word: faith is simply believing what God said, and acting like it's so. If I truly believe what God said, I will act like it's so. It's as simple as that.

It's not enough just to have faith. The word "faith" is a noun. "Believe" is a verb, and it depicts action. If I have faith, I'll know what God said, and I'll know that His words are imbued with the power to cause them to come to pass.

The Word of God is full of power (see Heb. 4:12). It's alive and active, and it is full of power. When the Word of God comes, it is looking for faith in the heart of the believer.

When faith is applied to the Word of God, a miracle always transpires. It is like the fertilization process in human reproduction. The woman provides the egg (or the embryo) and the man provides the sperm. When the sperm and the embryo come together, a life begins to take shape. It's the same with the Word of God and faith. God's Word contains all of His power (in an embryonic state), and it's there waiting. The minute faith comes, it germinates, and miracles are conceived.

When you were born again, you heard the Word of God, responded in your heart with faith, and it produced a miracle—your salvation. The Word took root, germinated, bore fruit and you were born again.

The apostles said, "Lord, increase our faith; help us to be able to believe and act on what you said."

Notice Jesus' response. It seems as if He ignored them. In fact, it almost seems as if He were rebuking them.

Jesus said (in Luke 17:6), "If ye have faith as a grain of mustard seed—."

The implication of His words was that they didn't have faith even the size of a mustard seed—the tiniest of seeds.

When I first studied this portion of the Scriptures, I understood Jesus' words as being a rebuke—that was, until I started having to face some of the same situations they were in. I had faith, but I couldn't understand how I ended up in some of the situations I managed to get myself into.

God never promised that we wouldn't have problems. In fact, if you look at the Book of Job, the very thing that brought Job to the devil's attention is the fact that he was blameless and upright, and he served God. The devil's accusation against God in the Book of Job shows that the devil knows more about God than most of God's people!

The devil said to God, "I have an accusation against Job." He actually had an accusation against God. He said, "God, you built the hedge around him, you prospered him, you gave him peace and you caused everything he has to increase." The devil was mad at God because Job was blessed. This was his accusation!

Most Christians don't see things this way. They think God steals, kills and destroys. It is almost as if they think the devil comes that they might have life and have it more abundantly! When you get blessed financially, they say, "Oh, that's the devil trying to pull you away from God." When you have a car accident, or lose someone you love, they may say, "Oh, God is trying to teach you something."

Since when did God and the devil change places? The Book of James says, "Let no man say when he is tempted, I am tempted of God: for God cannot be tempted with evil, neither tempteth he any man" (James 1:13).

The disciples, Jesus pointed out, had faith as a grain of mustard seed. Even so, they healed the sick, raised the dead, cast out devils, cleansed the lepers. They had faith, but they wanted more.

Jesus was saying that the way to increase your capacity for faith is by *using* what you have—by *doing* something. If you don't do anything, your capacity will never grow. By doing, you are planting your faith for the purpose of harvesting more faith.

A New Vocabulary

If I have faith, my vocabulary must change. Many of us hear the Word and we try to do it, but our vocabulary doesn't change. The words that come out of our mouths must be different from what they were before.

In our reading of the Scriptures we sometimes get confused by images and allegories. Jesus said, "Say to the tree to be uprooted." This may make some people think we need tree-moving faith or mountain-moving faith. But Jesus is not talking about literally moving trees. He is not trying to teach you how to cast a tree out of your yard! He is referring to something infinitely more important.

God speaks of things that are not as though they already were, but He does not speak of things that are as though they're not. Faith does not deny sickness. That is lying. If there is sickness in your body (the symptoms of illness and disease), faith does not say, "I'm not sick." Faith says, "Jesus bore my sicknesses and carried my diseases, and by His stripes I am healed."

In the face of financial difficulties, faith does not say, "I don't have a bill." Rather, faith says, "My God meets my every need according to His riches in glory by Christ Jesus."

Jesus said,

But which of you, having a servant
plowing or feeding cattle, will say
unto him by and by, when he is
come from the field, Go and sit
down to meat? And will not rather
say unto him, Make ready where-
with I may sup, and gird thyself,
and serve me, till I have eaten and
drunken; and afterward thou shalt
eat and drink? Doth he thank that
servant because he did the things
that were commanded him? I trow
not [or I think not]. So likewise ye,
when ye shall have done all those
things which are commanded you,
say, We are unprofitable servants:
we have done that which was our
duty to do" (Luke 17:7-10).

How does this teaching relate to faith? It
seems as if Jesus was rebuking them by saying, "If you had faith, you'd say—you'd begin to do." Then He said, "By the way,
which of you that has a servant, after the
servant finishes his work at the end of the
day, would tell your servant to sit down

and let me cook a meal for you?" He suggested that most of us would tell our servant, "Hey, get my food for me." Then, the servant having complied, we could sit down and eat.

Then Jesus said, "It should be the same with you and me. Once we've done all we are commanded to do, don't think anything of it, just say we've simply done our duty, or we've done that which we were supposed to do."

Isaiah 28 shows that faith comes line upon line, precept upon precept, here a little, there a little. The Old Testament tells me that God would drive out my enemies from before me, little by little. My faith grows from point A to point B to point C to point D. It keeps on growing. As I utilize my faith, my capacity for faith increases.

Once when I was preaching in Florida, I noticed that after every service the pastor of the church took about fifteen people out to eat. I thought, "This guy is generous! He's really blessing the people." One night I thought I would reciprocate by taking him and his wife out for dinner. I took them to a very nice steak house. I paid for the meal and thought, "Man, this guy has been such a blessing to his people and to me, this is the least that I can do."

Towards the end of the week, the pastor said, "Now, brother, I know you're a pilot. Would you like to go flying?"

I said, "Yeah, that would be great."

He went on, "We'll arrange it, and you can go up for an hour." He arranged it, and I went flying for an hour. It was wonderful.

I did not realize what was coming, however. When I went back to the hotel to check out on the last day, I noticed that the door to my room had been padlocked! A staff member explained, "It's past noon. The room was only covered till noon, and you have twenty dollars in phone bills that need to be paid." I proceeded to pay the phone bill, but as I was doing so, I wondered, "What's going on here?" No one mentioned a check-out time. If I had known, I would have asked for a late check-out and paid the bill in advance.

That evening, when I got to the meeting, the pastor said, "Praise the Lord, brother!

This is a tremendous meeting. Now, let's go over the finances."

I said, "Great!"

"This is how much came in." It was an astounding sum.

"Hallelujah!" I responded. "My faith IS working."

"This much came in," he explained," but, now your airfare...."

"My what?" I questioned incredulously.

"Your airfare was this amount...."

Reluctantly, I agreed, "Okay."

"And now the hotel bill was...."

I knew I had to speak up. "Do you mean I'm paying? You invited me to preach for you, and now I'm paying for my airfare and the hotel?"

He said, "Now, the meals."

I looked at the cost of the meals and responded, "What?" Finally, the truth dawned on me, That pastor hadn't been taking the fifteen people out to eat after every service. I had! He was being generous with *my* money!

He continued, "Then, our advertising costs were...." He proceeded to tell me more, "Now, it cost so much for you to fly today, so that leaves you with...." Believe me, there wasn't much left over! He then offered, "We have decided to be generous, however, and we've kicked in a couple of hundred dollars with it to bless you."

"Bless me? You robbed me!" I thought. Needless to say, I never went back there to preach.

On another occasion, as my wife was preparing for the delivery of one of our children, we received an entirely different kind of "blessing." A man walked up to me after one of the meetings and said, "Brother, God told me to give you a thousand dollars."

I thanked him and said, "Well, you can just put it in the offering."

"No, no, no. God said to give it to *you*." I was so glad that God had told him to give it to me. I was so grateful to God for this blessing.

Someone else at that meeting handed me a check for $500. It was wonderful. I went home with money for the hospital costs. I was rejoicing; I was praising God. In countless situations, God has been faithful to us.

God's people have been so good to us. To
be treated as I was by the pastor in Florida
is a rare experience, indeed.

EXERCISE YOUR FAITH

To increase your faith, begin to utilize
what you have. Do what you know to do.
Exercise your faith, step by step, point by
point.

I've had people laugh at me and taunt,
"You're not operating in faith." When that
happens, I look at where they are as com-
pared to where I am.

A friend of mine once felt his ministry
wasn't going as fast as he wanted it to go,
and he grew very upset about it. I pointed
out to him, "Look at Brother Hagin. It's tak-
en him forty years. But he went step by
step, and God brought him to the position
in which he now finds himself. Many ministries that shoot up overnight, fall overnight as well. Let's be sure to take it step
by step, so that when we get to wherever it
is that God has for us, we'll be able to main-
tain it. I don't want to be shot down."

"Lord, increase our faith," we pray. He will do so if we'll use what we've got first. Change what you say. Your vocabulary has to change. That which you know to do, you need to do. There are times when you need to stretch out. If you're used to giving five dollars, stretch yourself by giving ten. Be sure to use wisdom, however. We all need to learn to give sacrificially, but not foolishly.

The same thing is true when it comes to healing. In order to minister in healing, you have to keep at it. You need to keep pushing. Keeping on keeping on is necessary in order to break down the pressure of the enemy.

The power of faith is portrayed so vividly in Matthew 28:18: "And Jesus came and spake unto them, saying, All power is given unto me in heaven and in earth."

Isn't that a wonderful Scripture? "All power," Jesus said to His disciples.

> All power is given unto me in heaven and in earth. Go ye therefore, and teach all nations, baptizing them in the name of the Father, and of the Son, and of the Holy Ghost: Teaching them

to observe all things whatsoever I have commanded you: and, lo, I am with you alway, even unto the end of the world. Amen (Matt. 28:18-20).

Let's take a closer look at the context into which the Great Commission has been set. The focus of the passage begins in verse 16: "Then the eleven disciples went away into Galilee, into a mountain where Jesus had appointed them." Notice that this takes place after forty days. The Bible tells us that Jesus had appeared for forty days with many infallible proofs that He was the Christ. He walked through a wall. The disciples could feel the flesh of His hands. He wasn't vapor; He was flesh and blood. Even so, He was able to pass through material things.

He sat down and ate with His followers. Thomas put his hands in the holes of Jesus' hands, and in the gash in His side. The Lord had risen from the dead and the disciples were amazed. He spent forty days teaching them. Soon He would ascend into heaven. Ten days later the Holy Ghost would be sent.

Then the eleven disciples went away into Galilee, into a mountain where Jesus had appointed them. "And when they saw him, they worshiped him..." (Matt 28:17).

It is important to note that they saw Him. Clearly, if they saw Him and worshiped Him, they had to recognize Him. Indeed, they recognized who He was. They saw Him; they recognized Him; they worshiped Him. Standing before them was the One who was dead, and who is now alive, the One who defeated the devil, the One who gives resurrection life. Jesus defeated the power of the devil. He had defeated the last enemy—death—and He took its sting away. He proved that He was the risen Christ, the Lord of glory, and He was waiting to ascend to heaven. In spite of all this, the Scriptures say, "...but some doubted" (Matt. 28:17).

Can you imagine this response in the face of such miraculous power? Why did they doubt? Did they doubt that He was the Christ? No, not at all. There could not have been a shadow of doubt in their minds that He was the risen Christ. They knew, beyond all doubt, that He was Jesus, who had been crucified and was now risen from the dead. There could have been no doubt about that.

The word "doubt" literally means to be uncertain about which road to take. These men knew that Jesus was the Christ; they had to recognize that, but they were uncertain whether they wanted to follow in His footsteps. Surely they were excited over the fact that He was the risen Savior, but they could never forget what He went through to get there. They weren't quite sure they wanted to go through what He had to go through, because He had to die.

Likewise, you and I have to die. Paul said, "For me to live is Christ, and to die is gain" (Phil. 1:21).

These "doubters" did not want to die. They were at a crossroads. There were two roads they could have taken, but they doubted, and they didn't know which way to go. They were uncertain about which road to take. In the same way, we may recognize who Jesus is, but we may not be sure that we want to go His way because of all He had to go through. A measure of self-doubt is involved. We question ourselves, "Can I do what He did?"

How many of us are standing at the crossroads of faith? We may say, "Oh, that's wonderful, and I'm so thrilled and excited about those who are operating in faith. It's working for them, and they're doing thus-and-so, but I'm not sure I can do it. I'm not sure I want to pay the price."

"Yea, and all that will live godly in Christ Jesus shall suffer persecution" (2 Tim. 3:12). You will have to suffer persecution.

Some of our Christian brothers and sisters don't want to operate in faith, because they don't want to be "branded" as Word-of-Faith people. If they live a godly life, they're going to be persecuted anyway. You may as well be persecuted and have the benefits of faith, rather than be persecuted without its power.

"Well, we're not part of that prosperity cult," some will want to assure others.

Whether you are involved in the Faith movement or not, the world will think you're nuts simply because you're born again. Some people will want you to compromise about being filled with the Holy Ghost. If you compromise on that, they may want to get you to compromise on being born again, because, "You know, we don't like them born-again people around us because they're so different. They make me feel guilty."

We may as well face it, we will be persecuted in this life. We're not "hyper-faith people" even though some may try to put that label on us. Let's just walk out in faith, and walk away from the fear of man.

Yes, the disciples doubted. They were uncertain about which way to take. Notice how Jesus dealt with their uncertainty:

> And when they saw him, they worshipped him: but some doubted. And Jesus came and spake unto them, saying, All power is given unto me in heaven and in earth" (Matt. 28:17-18).

The Master simply said to them, "Listen, you're in doubt about which way to go: don't worry; this is the way to go. You

133

must simply *go* because I'm the One whose will and command must be obeyed in heaven and earth. You must simply go!"

STEP OUT IN FAITH

The best response to truth is to step out in faith. Once you do so, the power of God will be there to carry you through. The power of God will never be present to deliver you until you step out in faith. The added finances will never be there until you step out in faith. Healing will never come to the sick until you step out in faith. It won't be there until you do it.

Moses had to learn this lesson too. God told him, "You're going to deliver the people" (see Exod. 3). To defeat his doubts, Moses wanted a sign. God said, "I'll tell you what— I'll give you a sign. Once you have gone down and brought the children of Israel out, then you'll worship Me and serve Me on this mountain."

The sign was in the form of an action that Moses had to take. Once you've done everything," God assured him, "then you'll be back here." That is not the sign Moses wanted. He remonstrated with the Lord, "Give me some signs to prove it along the way."

God reiterated His message, "Here's the sign. You come back here when it's done. You'll worship Me here. That's the sign."

That's the answer that we all need to recognize. Once you step out in faith, the answer is there. Faith is not blind. We don't step out in blind faith, because faith sees clearly. In spite of the circumstances, faith enables us to clearly see what God says. Even so, most of us see the Word through the lenses of our circumstances. Instead of saying, "Nevertheless, at your Word . . . ," we say, "Nevertheless, in light of the circumstances . . . ." When nothing happens, we say, "See, I knew it. I told you so."

We have to step out in faith. When we step out in faith, we believe that what God said is true, and we act accordingly. When we believe it, and act in accordance with the Word, the power will always be there to carry it out. That which is necessary is always there for us. It will never be there, however, until we step out in faith.

Have you ever noticed that when you get sick and tired of being sick and tired, you're not sick and tired anymore? Have you ever noticed how, when it comes to healing, that it is when you finally say, "I've had it!" that the healing comes rapidly. At such times, you will likely say, "Why didn't I do that sooner?"

When you struggled about giving, for example, and you finally said, "In the name of Jesus, I will give . . . ," and you followed up by giving what He directed you to give; then it came back to you. Your response may have been, "Why didn't I do that sooner?"

When my wife lost her engagement ring soon after we were married, she began to pray in earnest for its safe return. I was making $25.00 a week at the time. The diamond in the ring was quite small, and we used to joke that you'd need a magnifying glass to see the stone. The ring cost only about $150. The stone was a diamond chip; it may actually have even been a chip off a chip!

She'd lost the ring once before, and then found it, and then she lost it again but didn't find it. She kept saying, "I'm believing God for a new diamond."

I said, "I'll agree with you."

She went on, "Really, I'm believing you'll buy me a new diamond." Then she described her preference for a one-carat diamond!

I told her, "Honey, if I get that amount of money in my hands, I will use it to pay bills!"

Nonetheless, for several years she kept on believing that I would buy it for her. And for years I kept telling her if that much money came, I would use it to pay bills.

One day she finally said, "That's enough! I'll agree with you for the diamond. I don't care how it comes. I'll just believe. I'm believing God for the diamond."

God had been dealing with her about another ring that she had. It was a beautiful ring. For eight or nine months God had been directing her to give that ring away. She didn't give in to His command throughout that period. Finally, she went up to the individual to whom she knew she was to give the ring and said, "You know, God has been dealing with me about something. Please forgive me for not doing this sooner. Here." She gave the ring to the lady.

Two days later we got a phone call. It was one of the ladies in the congregation who said, "Martha, please forgive me. I've been disobedient to God for over a year." She explained, "God has told me to do something. I've got to do it. Can I come over now?"

Martha said, "Sure, come on over."

When the woman came to our house, she opened a little box in front of Martha. She said, "Over a year ago God spoke to me about you when you were up on the platform. He said, *I want to bless my daughter because she's been faithful. I want you to give her your diamond pendant.*" The stone was a carat and a quarter in size!

For one year she had struggled with it. For eight months, likewise, my wife had struggled, too. The key to blessing came when my wife gave. Once my wife gave, the woman came to see it, and Martha's faith for a carat diamond was rewarded in abundance.

When she stepped out, it was accomplished. Martha told me what she'd been praying during those months. We'd agreed for a one-carat diamond, and she'd been praying, "Lord, I know we agreed for a carat, but, you know, just a little extra would be nice."

My wife has quite a taste for jewelry and clothing. Because she stepped out in faith, all I had to do was buy a new gold setting. That cost only $120. Until Martha stepped out, however, her miracle was withheld.

You may not have experienced the miracle that God wants for you because you've never stepped out in faith.

The disciples said, "Lord, increase our faith."

Jesus replied, "Use what you've got. Do something with it.

Stretch out, continue to do and be sure to change what you say."

6

Faith is a Tool

GOD STANDS BEHIND HIS WORD

God stands behind His Word in order to confirm His Word. I thank God that I don't have to stand behind His Word to confirm it. I thank God that He stands behind my words (when I speak in line with what He's saying), to confirm my words. What a joy it is to discover that when I speak what He says, He confirms it; when I speak what I say, He doesn't.

In similar manner, when I incur a bill because He said to, it gets paid. However, when I incur a financial obligation because

I came up with the idea, I pay it. (I have paid enough of them over the years, and I'm still paying on some!

Whatever God commands, He stands behind; but what He doesn't command, He doesn't stand behind. In Deuteronomy 28 we read, "And all these blessings shall come on thee, and overtake thee, if thou shalt hearken unto the voice of the Lord thy God" (Deut 28:2). In the same passage, we are admonished to "...observe and do all his commandments" (Deut 28:1). We have to observe and do, we have to do what God's command tells us to do—then we get the results we seek.

Notice God's strong word to His people: *All these blessings shall come upon thee, and—* the promise is powerful—*they'll overtake you.*

Has it ever happened to you like this? Have you ever experienced having the thing you were pursuing overtake you? Has anything you've ever chased after overtaken you? How can it overtake you if you're chasing after it? To overtake means to come up from behind and overwhelm.

"All these blessings shall come upon thee, and overtake thee, if you shalt hearken unto the voice of the Lord thy God" (Deut 28:2).

As I observe and do, I do so because He said to. I'm expecting these things to come upon me. I'm expecting them to overtake me. I'm not running after them; they're running after me. God said, "I'd be blessed in the city, I'd be blessed in the field."

Why are these wonderful promises my rightful inheritance? Because I'm observing to do, because I'm hearkening diligently to the voice of the Lord my God. I'm just doing what I've been told to do. And if I do what I've been told to do, I always get results.

It's time for you and me, as believers, to quit trying to get the results, and just to do what we've been told to do. The results automatically come because of Him who commanded them. We get the results because He commanded it, and take action because He commanded it.

THE BLESSING OF OBEDIENCE

It's time for us as believers to gather ourselves together, and join together in praying:

"Lord, we have blown it so much. We've been thinking we've been accomplishing some great things when all the time it was you who was accomplishing them. It's your Word. And as long as we walk in line with what you have directed us to do, you will bless us."

Such blessings are the result of obedience, the result of following the Master's directions.

God has said, "I want to bless you, and here are your directions for receiving the blessings." At Christmas time, my kids always got toys when they were little. Through my years of fatherhood, I've learned that when the box containing an unassembled toy gets to the house, I have to be sure to keep the directions. Have you ever tried to put something together when you didn't keep the directions. Do you remember what it's like when you have four or five pieces left over? You can't figure out where they go, so you have to go through the trash to find the directions.

I can't tell you the number of times when I've started to put something together without the directions. (Real men don't need directions, do they?) Every time I've taken this approach, I've had to go back and undo what I started, because I thought I knew what I was doing. But I didn't know what I was doing. I simply needed the manufacturer's directions.

Whenever this happened, and I found the directions, I had to undo my work, so that I could put the items together properly.

In every case, when I did what the directions told me to do, no parts were left over and nothing had to be undone. That which was supposed to be done was done.

The walk of faith is just like that. It's a matter of simply following the directions. It's a life style. "...The just shall live by faith" (Rom. 1:17). It's not a merit badge, nor is it a secret formula of some kind. And to the extent that we learn to live by faith, we will receive the blessings God has promised. As our faith grows, so do our blessings.

FOLLOW THE DIRECTIONS

Some people may be afraid to operate in faith because they don't want to do what they're told to do. If that is the case, they can never expect their faith to do what it's been told to do.

The disciples said, "Lord, increase our faith."

He answered, "Look, just use what you've got, and begin to change your vocabulary, and recognize that your faith has been given to you as a tool. Follow God's Word. Issue the commands that God has issued. Do what God says to do. Speak what God has said to speak, and watch the results."

"Nevertheless, at your word," Peter told the Lord when Jesus commanded him to lower his nets. Even though the fishermen had caught nothing all night long, Peter said, "Nevertheless, at your word." This is not magic. It is obedience responding to the faith produced by God's Word. It cannot fail because God has promised it, and He is always trustworthy. Whenever you act upon His Word in faith, as Peter did, you get results.

You and I are called to live by faith. The Word of God tells us that the just shall live by faith (Rom. 1:17). In Habakkuk, we read a similar declaration, "...the just shall live by his faith" (Hab. 2:4). When we put these two Scriptures together, we soon realize that we are the just, and that we must live by faith—the faith that God has given unto us. It is so important, therefore, for us to understand faith. People give various definitions of faith, but there is a very simple way of defining it; faith is simply believing what God said and acting like it is so.

If I believe what God said, and I act like it's so, then I'm operating in faith. My faith, then, involves believing what God said and acting as if it were so.

Our theme passage for this book is in Luke 17. Jesus' disciples asked Him to increase their faith level. These disciples are the same men Jesus gave authority to—authority to cast out devils, heal the sick, raise the dead and cleanse the lepers. These very individuals had done all these things; they had recognized where the source for such miracle-working power was to be found. Therefore, they came back to Jesus and said, "Lord, increase our faith. We're excited about what we've done, but we want to do even more."

We need to adopt that same militancy of spirit. Yes, we need to thank God for what has been accomplished, but we also need to know that it's time to do more. We can't continue on in what we did yesterday. I can't win today on what brought me victory yesterday. What brought me victory yesterday gives me a good foundation, increasing my hope and my expectation, but I can't win by what happened yesterday. I have to win by what I do today, and what I do tomorrow and what I do the day after that.

The disciples asked Jesus to increase their faith. How is someone's faith increased? How do we increase our capacity for faith? Faith comes by hearing, and hearing by the Word of God (see Rom. 10:17). As we hear the Word of God, faith comes.

Now, if "faith cometh by hearing," we must remember that "it stayeth by doing." Faith remains in the human heart by doing. Faith is our God-given tool for accomplishing His eternal purposes in our lives.

7

Change Your Way
of Speaking

For many years I would say, "O Lord, I'd
like to be just like brother Copeland." I
would marvel at how he just starts at one
Scripture and spends a whole week devel-
oping it! "How does he do it?" I would ask
myself. My answer finally came. The key
is to get full of the Word. When the Word
fills you, you are able to expound it, and
then it begins to come alive.

As we mentioned before, it sounded like
Jesus was rebuking His disciples when He
pointed out, "If ye had faith as a grain of
mustard seed..." (Luke 17:6). They had simply asked Him to increase their faith.

It's important for us to gain a clear perspective on this passage. Jesus wasn't trying to accuse them of not having any faith. These were the ones who had raised the dead. They had cast out devils, cleansed the lepers, healed the sick, and so forth. Surely they had faith. They believed the words of Jesus, and they acted on the words of Jesus.

Imagine this group of illiterate fishermen when Jesus turned to them and said, "Okay, now I want you to go out and heal the sick. I want you to go out and raise the dead. I want you to go and cleanse the lepers." (No one touched lepers in those days!) He went on, "I want you to do these things and preach the good news, telling others that the Kingdom of God is at hand."

They responded with obedience and preached that the Kingdom of God was at hand. They spoke forth their faith with words such as these: "The power of God is available here today, and we'll prove it to you. Bring the sick to us." And it worked. They believed the words of Jesus, and they acted on His Word. They changed their way of speaking.

Jesus did not rebuke His disciples when they asked Him to increase their faith. He told them how to do so. He showed them how to speak their faith—to command their faith—to use their faith.

He said, 'This is how you increase your capacity. If you had faith as a grain of mustard seed, you'd say to this tree . . . ." In other words, the way you increase your capacity for faith is by doing what you have heard. In effect, the Master was saying, "Since you have faith, make it like that mustard seed by planting it and using it."

He told them how to use it: "If you had faith, you would say . . . ."

If we are going to operate in faith, we must change our vocabulary. We have to change the way we speak in order to operate in faith. Usually people don't like to hear that. Most of us detest change of any kind. We want to talk the way we always have. We want to call things that are as though they are not. But such an approach will not take us far in our faith walk. With such an attitude, nothing in our lives will change.

JUSTIFIED BY FAITH

Over the past few years, within the Body of Christ, we seem to have been thinking that because we are operating in faith, we have the right to certain things. We approach God with the attitude, "If I confess it enough, if I pray enough, if I listen to enough tapes.... All I have to do is all these things, and I will get thus and so."

There is some truth in this. You will get "thus and so," but it is not because you have earned these things. It is because God promised them to you. You receive what God has promised simply because He promised it. Your actions are a result of the promise God has given.

Some people get turned on to the Word of Faith message and they try to find out how to get a million dollars overnight! Is this the scriptural approach?

God gives me a promise, and I receive that promise by faith. God says, "I am going to give you salvation." We receive the free gift of eternal life through faith. "For by grace are ye saved through faith; and that not of yourselves: it is a gift of God: Not of works, lest any man should boast" (Eph. 2:8-9). God moves in the same way whenever He responds to our faith.

It's the grace of God; the faith of God goes into operation. I do not deserve it, but God gives it to me. God gives it to me in spite of the fact that I don't deserve it. If I deserved it, He wouldn't give it to me, but because I don't deserve it, He gives it to me. Therefore, it becomes mine.

Too many Christians spend all their time trying to deserve what God gives them, because they know they don't deserve it. We try to make ourselves worthy so that God will give us something. The minute you make yourself worthy to receive what He would give you, He can't give it to you. God does not give you what you earn. He gives you what you don't earn.

Jesus has been made unto us wisdom, righteousness, sanctification and redemption. (See 1 Cor. 1:30.) "Therefore if any man be in Christ, he is a new creature: old things are passed away; behold, all things are become new" (2 Cor. 5:17). Through

Jesus Christ, I've been made the righteousness of God. I am not becoming the righteousness of God. I am being sanctified. My life style is changing; holiness is ongoing; and I am righteous by virtue of the new birth. I didn't do anything to deserve righteousness. I was a sinner, but "God commendeth his love toward us, in that, while we were yet sinners, Christ died for us" (Rom. 5:8).

JUSTIFIED IN WHAT I SAY

When I received Jesus, God said, "You, Mike Landsman, are righteous!" I didn't look righteous. I didn't feel righteous, but I am the righteousness of God in Christ Jesus. Many times, I thought I was lying about this, but I found a verse of Scripture that reassured me, "...let God be true, but every man a liar;... That thou mightest be justified in thy sayings, and mightest overcome when thou art judged" (Rom 3:4).

This passage teaches that when it comes down to a conflict between what you say and what God says, you can be sure that

God is true. Anything that is contrary to what God said is, therefore, a lie. This certainly enables us to be justified in what we say.

I'm justified in what I say when I say what God says, because what He says is true. Jesus said, "If you had faith the size of a grain of a mustard seed, you would say...." You'd change your vocabulary to say what God said, because what God said is true. What someone else says is all too often contrary to God's Word. If God says I am righteous, then I can declare that I am righteous.

This is important to understand. The minute you say, "I'm not righteous," you're calling God a liar! An egotistical person is someone who will take nobody else's word but their own. Egotists are proud individuals.

In contrast, a humble individual is someone who receives the word of someone else with a teachable spirit. A humble individual says, "Jesus is made unto me wisdom, right-eousness, sanctification and redemption. By my faith in Christ, I have been made the righteousness of God; therefore, I am righteous by my faith in Him." That is true humility.

Ego and pride say, "Oh, I'm just a worm." A person who makes such a statement wants to appear to be humble, but he or she is actually proud. Romans 3:4 says, "Let God be true and every man a liar." If God said you have been made righteous, you can say it, too—and believe it—and act upon it!

A modern translation of Romans 3:4 concludes with: " . . . and overcome when you are condemned." How can I overcome when I am condemned? By saying what God says. This is possible because God is true, and everybody else is a liar. If God says I am right-eous, then I will be justified in what I say. I will overcome when they condemn me; realizing that others may condemn me because they just don't understand. Their false humility, which is actually pride, leads them to say things that they have no knowledge of. Such deception has been passed down from generation to generation, and without realizing it, many people have refused to take God at His Word. They have no problem with taking "Brother so-and-so" at his word; they'll take the church fathers at their word, but they won't take the Word of Almighty God at face value. Such people are truly deceived.

THE HEDGE OF PROTECTION

When I was in college, I took a course on the Book of Job. My teacher spent a whole semester proving to us that Job's problem was his mouth; he showed that Job operated in fear.

We often hear it said that God built a hedge of protection around Job. (See Job 1:10.) It was actually Satan who talked about "the hedge of protection." God did not mention it, because God never builds a hedge around anyone. God gives you all the hedge-building material, but you've got to put it up. God gives you everything for the hedge, but if you don't put it up, He won't build it for you! Whenever you operate in fear, you pull the hedge of protection down.

The Book of Ezekiel gives us further insights into this truth. God said, "And I sought for a man among them, that should make up the hedge, and stand in the gap before me for the land . . ." (Ezek. 22:30). God didn't say that He made up the hedge; He said that He looked for an individual who would stand in the gap and make up the hedge. We need to change our vocabulary. This will help to build God's protective hedge around us.

Many critics of the Faith Movement will suggest that we do what we do in order to become something we're not or to get something we don't have. That's not the case at all. I don't do things in order to become; I do because I already am. I do not give in order to get; I give because God said, "Give and it shall be given unto you." Therefore, when I give, I expect to receive a return. I count it as done. It's not because I'm giving to get, but simply because my Father said, "If you give, this is what I will do." It's not that I deserve it because of my actions; it's just because God said that's the way it's done.

So much of what we do is rooted in our attitudes; it stems from our motives. Most Christians spend all of their lives trying to become what they already are. Is it surprising, then, that when they are in need of healing, they don't receive? Many will go up to the prayer line, have hands laid on them, but they really don't expect to receive healing, because of past failures and sins. Their thinking goes something like this, "God couldn't possibly heal me, because I don't deserve it."

When Abraham Lincoln gave the greatest and most memorable speech of his life—the Gettysburg Address—no one responded to it with positive comments at first. They thought that it was a complete failure.

Because of this, Lincoln himself came to think that the speech at Gettysburg was a failure. Nonetheless, it went down in history as one of the greatest speeches ever. The problem was that Lincoln interpreted the lack of response as being negative; he believed his erroneous perception, and therefore, he believed that he had failed when, in actuality, his address was a profound success!

> For what saith the scripture? Abraham believed God, and it was counted unto him for righteousness. Now to him that worketh is the reward not reckoned of grace, but of debt. But to him that worketh not, but believeth on him that justifieth the ungodly, his faith is counted for righteousness (Rom 4:3-5).

Righteousness is not reckoned according to what you do; you don't do righteous things to earn God's blessings or to deserve them, but you do righteous things because God promised righteousness to you. He has already given it to you; therefore, you act in righteous ways.

Notice what the Apostle Paul points out, "Therefore it is of faith, that it might be by grace..." (Rom 4:16). Grace is God's unmerited, undeserved favor. Therefore, it is of faith that it might be by God's unmerited favor, "...to the end the promise might be sure..." (Rom. 4:16).

Faith says, "I see it; I recognize it—but God says...." Too often people take a different approach. Their confession may be, "Yes, Father, I see what you say; I recognize what you say, but the circumstances...." We've gone at it backwards. Such reverse thinking leads to doubt: "I know what your Word says, Lord, but you don't understand. I know that you said, 'Give and it shall be given unto you,' but...I know that you said you'd meet my every need according to your riches in glory in and by Christ Jesus, but how am I going to pay this bill?" What could have been faith has now become reasoning.

We grow weak in faith, giving glory to the problem. Instead of recognizing the problem and saying, "Yes, I see it. That's a bill that's got to be paid. Father, you said you'd meet my every need according to your riches in glory in and by Christ Jesus. I see this bill; I see what it says; nevertheless, I know what you have said, and I've never seen the righteous forsaken, nor his seed begging for bread. Therefore, I call that bill paid in Jesus' name."

Please don't misunderstand me on this crucial point. I don't want you to infer that

I mean that you should write a hot check. Rather, call that bill paid, and then do something. If I've got some money in my pocket, but not enough to pay that bill, I will find some place to "plant" that money quickly. Let me give you an example.

"DEVIL, YOU'RE SO DUMB!"

As an associate pastor in Southern California in the late seventies, I was getting ready to go to Brother Hagin's Camp Meeting near Tulsa, Oklahoma, along with my wife. We were very excited about the trip, so we were praising God because we'd believed God for the finances to go, and we had enough money to cover our round-trip airfare. Our tickets were the "supersaver" kind, the kind you can't cancel. If you don't go, you lose all your money.

We also had enough money to pay for one night's hotel accommodations. We had to pay for one night in advance in order to hold our room. The problem was we had nothing left over. We kept on believing God, however, as the time of our departure approached.

We thanked God for meeting our every need, for providing us with the money for our vacation, including meals and lodging. We had determined how much money we wanted to give (in the meetings) in advance. We said, "We thank you that we have X-amount to be able to give. And not only that, Father, but we have the ability to buy all the tapes and books we want, and to be able to bless other people, and take other people out to eat." We claimed all these blessings in the name of Jesus.

With only one week to go, I had one hundred dollars worth of bills facing me. My checkbook balance showed only four dollars. I also had four dollars in my pocket! One Sunday morning, a week before our planned departure, I began to fear that we would not be able to go. What a great vacation it could be—rest, excitement, fellowship and faith-building experiences! But I could not get around the fact that I had a salary check coming, but the salary check would be only enough to pay those bills!

A good part of this onslaught of negative thinking took place during the Sunday morning offering. Thank God, I knew His Word. In my heart, I said, "Devil, you are so dumb. I'll tell you what I'm going to do! I'm going to take the four dollars in my pocket and put them in the offering. That's what I'm going to do!"

He challenged, "All you have is eight dollars; you can't even pay your bills!"

The minute I said, "I'm going to put the four dollars in the offering," my thinking changed, however, and all my thought patterns changed as well.

My mind continued to be bombarded, "Don't do that; you need that to pay your bills." Right then, I started to laugh. I don't know what the people in the area thought of me, but I started to laugh. In my mind, I said, "Devil, you are so dumb. You're telling me eight dollars can't pay a hundred dollars worth of bills, and now here I say I'm going to give four dollars, and you're telling me I can't do that because I need the four dollars to pay my hundred dollars worth of bills? Four dollars never paid a hundred dollars worth of bills. You can't stretch it that way. You're so dumb!"

I gave all my pocket money, then I rejoiced and I was so happy! That night, when we went back to church, someone rushed up to my wife and said, "Oh, here; excuse me, here, here, I've got to give this to you." It was a gift of one hundred and some odd dollars. God had spoken to this individual during the morning service that day! We had enough money to tithe. (I always take the first ten percent off for God. Then I get to give even more!)

We had enough to give; we had enough for the first things. We had the money to pay all those bills. Still, however, I had one week to go before the scheduled vacation was to commence. There was no more money! Our senior pastor was going to the camp meeting, too. He said, "Isn't it going to be great? We're going to be in Tulsa, man, it's going to be tremendous; we're going to have a great time."

I replied, "Yes, we're looking forward to it. Hallelujah!"

My wife and I continued to stand in faith. The senior pastor went to Tulsa early. During the Wednesday night service, I was scheduled to preach, and our prayer coordinator was to receive the offering and lead the other parts of the service.

She got up and said, "How many of you appreciate Pastor Mike and his wife?"

Everybody responded, "Yes, hallelujah!"

She went on, "Good. How many of you know it's his birthday this weekend? We want to do something special for his birthday, don't we? I've already talked with the pastor, and we're going to receive an offering to bless him for his birthday."

I was truly shocked. I knew they had always received an offering for the senior pastor—birthdays, anniversaries, Christmas, housewarmings, etc. (Those were some of the benefits of being the senior pastor.) But they had never done this for the associate pastor!

I began to think, "This is great!" She then proceeded with the offering, "And we're going to receive that offering for Mike and Martha first."

At this point, two thoughts went through my mind. Number one, I was excited because I knew the first offering was always the biggest. Secondly, I believed that God was at work to meet our needs. Usually the guest speaker gets what's left. We need to take care of the local church, because if the local church wasn't there, the guest speaker wouldn't have any place to minister!

She took the offering, and we were blessed! There was enough money for us to pay for the rest of our hotel expenses, our transportation while we were there, whatever we wanted to eat whenever we wanted to eat it, and even enough to take people out to dinner. We didn't have to eat at fast-food restaurants; we could go to more expensive places. Now we had the money we needed, not only to give the amount we had determined beforehand, but even more than what we had determined! And there was enough left over to enable us to buy tapes and books for ourselves, as well as some tapes for other people. We were able to go out and buy the things we wanted, and we came home with money in our pocket! All from that one offering.

Incidentally, the second offering was the largest offering the church had ever received in a midweek service! I report all this just to remind you that when we try to figure things out, we often miss God's plan.

The devil had said, "How are you going to pay that hundred dollar's worth of bills when you only have eight dollars?"

"I'm going to give," I determined in my heart.

"Oh, no, you can't do that," he warned.

We must never forget that faith speaks of things that are not as though they were. Faith enables you to change your vocabulary and your style of living. It helps you to learn to speak of things that are not as though they already were. But remember, you don't speak of things that are as though they're not. This is an important distinction to keep in mind.

Abraham firmly considered the circumstances. He didn't deny them or try to avoid them. He said, "But, God, I recognize that I'm a hundred years old. I recognize that Sara is ninety years old. I recognize that I'm past the age for siring children and Sara's past the age for bearing children." While recognizing the reality of the circumstances, however, he said, "Yet God said and God promised." He staggered not at the promise of God through unbelief, but was strong in faith, giving glory to God, believing that He which had promised was truly able to fulfill His promise.

Abraham believed what God said. He said, "I recognize the circumstances and the situations, but God said...."

We have a tendency to recognize what God said, and then say, "But look at the circumstances...." This is a reversal of the biblical approach. We must recognize the circumstances. Faith doesn't jump into things without recognizing reality. But faith also says, "Now God said thus and so, so I'd better be doing thus and so, because God said it."

Always be sure to act on your faith in accord with what God has said, not according to what someone else has said God said. Second-hand knowledge will get you nowhere. God doesn't have any grandkids; He only has kids. I can tell you what God says, but then you need to go back and find out for sure that God said it. Then, when you act on it, you act on it because God said to.

Whenever the devil starts to give me a hard time, I like to remind him that there was a time when he thought he had won—when he took Jesus to hell. I also like to remind him of what happened after that. I will say to him, "Remember on the cross, devil? Ha, ha, you thought you had Him. Remember those three days and three nights? You were rejoicing, because you had killed the Messiah, or you thought you had. Then you remember how He stripped you of all your power and authority? I want to remind you of that. Not only did He strip you of it, but on His way up, He gave me the keys. Ha, ha."

The devil doesn't like it when I talk like that. He doesn't like it when you talk that way either. That's why he doesn't get upset when you say, "Oh, if God would only stretch down His hand from heaven, and see fit in His mercy and grace and love to but impart a healing touch unto me. Lord, just a touch from your hand, please."

I don't want just a touch. I want what I don't deserve—complete healing, complete prosperity. I want what I don't deserve because God wants to give it to me. Because God gave it to me, it's mine. It's my legal birthright.

The things we have are ours by right of the new birth, which is something we didn't earn or deserve. It was freely given to us by God even though we didn't deserve it. In the same way, all these other blessings come to us, even though we don't deserve them. It's part of being in the family.

When my young son wants a drink of apple juice, he never asks me if he can get some apple juice out of the refrigerator; he simply goes to the refrigerator and gets the apple juice, because he's thirsty. He wants it and needs it. He doesn't have to ask me if he can have the apple juice that's in the refrigerator, because it's in the house where he lives. It's there for him to use and enjoy. These privileges are a part of my children's inheritance. The things that are in the house belong to them.

When my wife was pregnant with our first child, I began to help her by clearing the table and rinsing the dishes. After she delivered our first son, however, a couple of months later, I did not do these chores and she remarked, "Well?"

I replied, "What do you mean by 'Well'?"

"You didn't clear the table and rinse the dishes."

"Was I supposed to?"

She said, "Yes, you did it back then." It became my responsibility from then on. That is, until my children took over! Ah, the blessings of children!

The disciples said, "Lord, increase our faith" (Luke 17:5). Jesus replied,

> If ye had faith as a grain of a mustard seed, ye might say unto this sycamine tree, Be thou plucked up by the root, and be thou planted in the sea; and it should obey you (Luke 17:6).

You would say, and it would obey! We have to change the way we speak. Our vocabularies have to change. God expects us to speak differently if we're going to learn to operate in faith.

You will be persecuted when this change

takes place in your life. You will be attacked by the devil, both through circumstances and through people. The devil may even attack you through Brother and Sister Christian—believers who do not have the understanding you have. Some Christians will try to get you to live below your rights and privileges. When they say you can't have what you are believing, it's because they don't want to do what is necessary to receive it for themselves.

"Yea, and all that will live godly in Christ Jesus shall suffer persecution" (2 Tim. 3:12). It's part of the program. The important question to ask yourself in the face of this reality is: "Are you going to suffer persecution as a blessed person, or are you going to suffer persecution like everybody else does?" The latter alternative leads to self-pity and defeat. "Oh, poor me. I don't know why God is doing this to me. I just don't know what the Lord is trying to teach me."

It certainly isn't that God is trying to teach you that you're supposed to be healthy. He's trying to teach you that

173

you're supposed to be blessed, having enough to meet every need.

TRUSTING GOD

So many people have a weird view of faith. They expect everything to be there before they have the need. God never promised that. He did say, "I'll meet your every need," however.

Our confidence, our trust and our rest rely on the fact that when we have a need, God said He'd meet it. He promises to supply all our needs. I don't have to have it in my hand to know that it will be met. But I know that it will be met because He said it would be. Therefore, my confidence is in His reliability, faithfulness and trustworthiness. The truth of His Word enables me to trust Him.

I need to trust more than I need to try. "Let us labour therefore to enter into that rest..." (Heb. 4:11). How do we labor to enter into rest? The statement almost seems to be a contradiction in terms.

The very next verse shows us how it happens. "For the word of God is quick [alive] and powerful, and sharper than any two-edged sword..." (Heb. 4:12).

We labor to enter into rest by confessing the Word, and this means by changing our vocabularies. My labor is in changing the vocabulary I have by beginning to speak what God says. When I speak what God says, in the way that God says it, I am doing my part (performing my labor). Then I enter into rest because God said He'd accomplish whatever is needed; therefore, He will do it!

I can't do it. If I could do it, I would earn it. I can't earn it; I don't deserve it; but God does it. It comes by faith. I cease from my labors. After I speak what God says, then I stand fast in that. Then I have confidence and rest in saying, "Now you said it, Father; it's up to you to do it."

Jesus showed this to His disciples when they requested, "Lord, increase our faith." They wanted Him to increase their capacity for believing. He revealed to them that they needed to use what they had by changing their vocabulary.

In the same way, we must begin to say what God says.

175

Faith is your servant, a tool for you to utilize. By using this God-given tool—by speaking His Word—your faith increases automatically. This is God's will for you!

Epilogue

In our daily walk with the Lord and in endeavoring to have an impact on the world, we must continue to grow in every area of our lives. The truths that I have presented in this book are by no means all that you need to mature in God—they are my own personal contributions to your spiritual maturation.

I am convinced that the church has not yet seen its finest hour. We are learning and growing at a tremendous rate. The Lord is building a glorious church that has much to do in reaching the lost and establishing His rule and reign on the earth.

The desire to increase our faith is for the purpose of meeting the needs of a suffering humanity. If we do not deliver the truth to them, who will? We must stretch beyond our petty, self-imposed borders and impact the world. It will take all of us going beyond our abilities and relying on God's ability to get the job done. We must be of a mind to conquer and subdue the god of this present age and lay the kingdoms of this world at the feet of our God.

It is to that end that I have written this book, and I hope that you have been inspired to step out boldly for God.

Available from Michael Landsman Ministries:

Single Tapes ($5.00)

Plain Brown Wrapper
  (Marital Sex)
Lord, Increase Our Faith
The Attitude of a Servant
"Dating" is not "Mating"
Who Am I?
Sanctification
The Name of Jesus

Two-Tape Series ($10)

Prevailing Patience
Possessed and Moved
  by God
Peace in the Midst
  of Turmoil

Three-Tape Series ($15)

Lord, Increase Our Faith
Are You Bearing Fruit?
Positive Power of
  Resistance
Praise, Strength, Spice,
  and Fire
Commanding Power
  of Faith
Supportive Ministries I
Supportive Ministries II
Relationship, Not Religion
The Christian Family
How to Hear God Speak
Looking at the Real You
Husbands, Love Your
  Wives

Four-Tape Series ($20.00)

The Necessity of Change
The Mercy of God

12-Tape Series ($60.00)

Faith Foundations
Healing in the Atonement

Videos ($20.00)

Attitude of a Servant
Faith Foundations (6 videos,
2 messages each—$150.00)
God Will Not Afflict
Lord, Increase Our Faith
Plain Brown Wrapper
The Mercy of God
Principles of
  Administration
Who Am I?

Other Materials Available:

- World Outreach Corres-
  pondence Bible School
- Tape of the Month Club
  ($5.00)
- Honolulu University—
  External Degree
  Programs

*To obtain any of these materails
or to inquire about Dr. Landsman's travel itinerary, please
contact:*

**Michael Landsman
Ministries
P.O. Box 865
So. Plainfield, NJ 07080**